개정판

Let's English

기초생활영어

Kim Soo Jung

Profile

김수정 Kim Soo Jung

인하공업전문대학 항공운항과 졸업
한국방송통신대학교 영어영문학과 졸업
Hospitality Management Diploma at AHLA Hotel Business School
성균관대학교 번역/TESOL 대학원 TESOL학과 석사

경력

싱가포르항공 객실승무원
대한항공 객실승무원
Certified Hospitality Department Trainer at American Hotel & Lodging Educational Institute
HSBC 은행 Quality Assurance Officer
현) 아세아항공전문학교 항공운항학부 교수
항공서비스포럼 회원
한국영어교육학회(KATE) 회원

저 서 English for Flight Attendants(2012, 백산출판사)
e-mail kimsisle@naver.com

Let's English (기초생활영어)

2013년 10월 31일 초 판 1쇄 발행
2016년 3월 10일 개정판 1쇄 발행

지은이 | 김수정
펴낸이 | 김종욱
펴낸곳 | 지식인
등 록 | 제301-2013-134호
주 소 | 서울시 도봉구 도봉로 476, 415호(삼성쉐르빌퍼스티)
전 화 | 02)2266-8606(대)
팩 스 | 02)2266-8607
이메일 | jisikin2013@naver.com
홈페이지 | www.jisikinbook.co.kr

ISBN 978-89-98591-11-3 (93740)

값 19,000원 (CD 포함)

Let's English
기 초 생 활 영 어

PREFACE

대학생들에게 강의하면서 가장 많이 듣는 질문은 바로, "어떻게 하면 영어를 잘할 수 있나요?"입니다.

대학생들뿐만 아니라, 거의 모든 이들에게 있어 영어는 생각만 하면 가슴 답답해지는 밀린 숙제와도 같은 것이 아닌가 합니다.

하지만 모든 학문이 그러하듯 영어에도 왕도는 없습니다. 최소한 1년 가까이 꾸준한 노력을 통해 반복학습을 해야 하며, 꾸준히 지속적으로 노력하는 사람이 잘하는 것이지 머리 좋은 사람이 잘하는 것이 아닙니다.

학생들과 영어에 대한 얘기를 나누다보면 많이 듣게 되는 말 중에 하나가, "저는 눈으로 보면 알겠는데, 말이 안 떨어져요.", "매일 20개씩 영어단어를 외우고 있어요."입니다.

영어는 몸으로 익히는 기술입니다. 실제로 운동장에 나가 공을 차야지, 화면으로 박지성의 플레이만 눈으로 봐서는 절대로 축구를 잘할 수 없는 것과 같은 이치입니다.

이번에 제가 집필한 Let's English는 영어의 기초가 부족한 성인 영어학습자 및 기존 한국의 문법 및 읽기교육에 익숙해 있는 학생들을 위해서 기획되었습니다. 기초가 부족한 분들도 혼자서 부담 없이 할 수 있는 한국어 설명이 자세하게 곁들여 있으며, 아울러 실제 이 책을 통해 학습하는 분들이 상황에 따른 다양한 영어표현을 기초부터 차근차근 배움으로써 기본이 되는 표현들을 익힌 후에, 실제 상황에 맞는 생활영어를 응용할 수 있게끔 충분한 양의 연습문제를 수록하였습니다.

영어단어를 많이 외웠다고 해서 독해나 회화를 잘할 수 있는 것이 아니기 때문에, 여기서는 영어의 기초를 다지기 위한 문법 맛보기 파트를 시작으로 해서 20대 초반의 한국인 유학생이 미국에서 겪는 일상생활을 바탕으로 한 생활영어 표현의 대화문들로 구성하였습니다. 문장 내용의 상황을 머릿속에서 상상하면서 단어보다는 문장으로 암기를 해야 살아있는 영어 공부가 되기 때문입니다.

또한 교재에서 제공되는 CD를 활용하여 듣고 따라읽는 연습을 하고, 다양한 상황의 롤플레이와 액티비티를 통해 암기한 지식을 반복연습을 통해 체득함으로써 살아있는 다양한 의사소통 활동에 참여할 수 있게끔 하였습니다.

영어는 하기 나름입니다. 영어를 해야겠다는 절실한 마음과 여러분의 노력에 따라 성과는 천차만별입니다. 머뭇거리거나 실수를 두려워하지 말고, 어린 아이가 말을 배우듯 복잡하게 생각하지 않고 그저 열심히 따라하기만 해보세요.

모쪼록 저의 마음이 여러분들에게 다가가 이 책으로 인해 영어회화와 영미문화에 흥미를 갖게 되었으면 좋겠습니다. 이제까지 물심양면으로 도움을 주신 아세아항공전문학교 교직원분들, 제 수업에 함께 한 수많은 학생들, 그리고 지식인출판사 편집부에 감사의 말씀을 드립니다.

끝으로, 직장생활과 학업, 육아 등으로 지쳐있는 제게 늘 힘이 되어주는 가족, 그리고 힘들 때마다 곁에 있어주는 삶의 동반자인 남편과 사랑하는 딸 Kate에게 이 책을 선물합니다.

김수정

CONTENTS

Ⅰ. 파닉스(Phonics)

【1】 알파벳 기본 소리값

Alphabets(알파벳)	Name(이름)	Sound(소리)	Words(단어)
A a	에이	/애/	ant, apple, arrow
B b	비이	/브/	baby, ball, book
C c[1]	씨이	/크/	cat, car, cup
D d	디이	/드/	desk, dog, doctor
E e	이-	/에/	egg, end, energy
F f	에프	/프f/	fish, fan, food
G g[2]	쥐이	/그/	game, garden, gift
H h[3]	에이취	/흐/	ham, hand, hiking
I i	아이	/이/	ink, ill, igloo
J j	줴이	/쥐/	jam, jump, juice
K k	케이	/크/	key, kite, kitchen
L l	엘	/르/	lemon, lock, lion
M m	엠	/므/	milk, monkey, music
N n	엔	/느/	nut, number, nose
O o	오우	/아/	owl, out, octopus
P p	피이	/프/	pig, pizza, pan
Q q	큐	/쿼/	question, quiz, queen
R r	얼	/뤄r/	red, ribbon, rain
S s[4]	에쓰	/쓰/	sun, sand, seesaw
T t	티이	/트/	tiger, tent, toy
U u	유우	/어/	umbrella, up, under
V v	뷔이	/브v/	violin, vegetable, van
W w	더블유	/워/	water, web, window
X x[5]	엑스	/크스/	box, six, fox
Y y	와이	/여/	yes, yoyo, yellow
Z z	지이	/즈z/	zoo, zebra, zipper

✔ 주황색으로 표시된 a, e, i, o, u는 모음이며, 위에 표기된 발음은 단모음(short vowels)으로 발음될 때의 소리값입니다.

【2】 단모음(Short Vowels)

1) 단모음 A a /애/

단모음 a와 다른 알파벳을 붙여서 소리를 만들어 봅시다.

ag	애 + 그 ► 액	am[6]	애 + 음 ► 앰
an[7]	애 + 은 ► 앤	ap	애 + 프 ► 앺
at	애 + 트 ► 앹		

앞에 여러 가지 자음을 넣어 연습해 봅시다.

ex) bag, jam, can, map, cat

2) 단모음 E e /에/

단모음 e와 다른 알파벳을 붙여서 소리를 만들어 봅시다.

ed	에 + 드 ► 엗	eg	에 + 그 ► 엑
en	에 + 느 ► 엔	et	에 + 트 ► 엩

앞에 여러 가지 자음을 넣어 연습해 봅시다.

ex) bed, red, leg, ten, pen, jet, net

3) 단모음 I i /이/

단모음 i와 다른 알파벳을 붙여서 소리를 만들어 봅시다.

---

1 c는 주로 /크/라는 소리값을 가지지만 부드럽게 /쓰/라는 소리가 나기도 합니다. 예) circle, circus

2 g는 /그/ 소리 외에도 /쥐이-/ 소리가 날 때도 있습니다. 예) giant, giraffe, gym
또, sign /사인/처럼 묵음인 경우도 있습니다.

3 h는 보통 /흐/ 소리가 나지만, 때로는 묵음인 경우도 있습니다. 예) hour, honest

4 s 뒤에 다른 자음이 와서 이중자음이 되면 발음을 누그러뜨려 /스/ 소리를 냅니다. 예) smile, snail

5 x는 주로 단어의 맨 끝에서 /크스/로 소리나지만, 단어의 앞머리에 쓰이거나 모음과 만날 때는 또다른 소리를 가집니다.
① 단어의 앞머리에선 /엑스/ 예) X-ray
② ex로 시작할 땐 /그즈/ 예) exam, exit

6 모음 뒤에 m이 오면 /므/가 아닌 /음/의 소리값으로 변하여 미음 받침과 같은 역할을 합니다.

7 모음 뒤에 n이 오면 /느/가 아닌 /은/의 소리값으로 변하여 니은 받침과 같은 역할을 합니다.

id	이 + 드 ► 읻	ig	이 + 그 ► 익
in	이 + 느 ► 인	ip	이 + 프 ► 잎
it	이 + 트 ► 잍		

앞에 여러 가지 자음을 넣어 연습해 봅시다.

ex) kid, pig, pin, lip, hit

4) 단모음 O o /아/

단모음 o와 다른 알파벳을 붙여서 소리를 만들어 봅시다.

og	아 + 그 ► 악	op	아 + 프 ► 앞
ot	아 + 트 ► 앝	ox	아 + 크스 ► 악스

앞에 여러 가지 자음을 넣어 연습해 봅시다.

ex) jog, fog, mop, top, hot, pot, fox, box

5) 단모음 U u /어/

단모음 u와 다른 알파벳을 붙여서 소리를 만들어 봅시다.

ug	어 + 그 ► 억	up	어 + 프 ► 엎
um	어 + 음 ► 엄	un	어 + 은 ► 언
ut	어 + 트 ► 엍		

앞에 여러 가지 자음을 넣어 연습해 봅시다.

ex) mug, cup, gum, sun, cut

【3】 장모음(Long Vowels)

장모음은 '길게 소리나는 모음'입니다. 단어가 e로 끝나면 앞에 있는 모음의 소리가 긴 소리(알파벳 이름 그대로)로 변하게 됩니다.

1) 장모음 A a /에이/

장모음 a와 다른 알파벳을 붙여 소리를 만들어 봅시다.

ake	에이 + 크 ► 에잌	ame	에이 + 음 ► 에임
ane	에이 + 은 ► 에인	ape	에이 + 프 ► 에잎
ate	에이 + 트 ► 에잍		

앞에 여러 가지 자음을 넣어 연습해 봅시다.

ex) cake, name, cane, tape, gate

2) 장모음 E e /이-/

모음 e는 다른 모음과 만나지 않고 혼자서 소리가 길어질 때도 있습니다.
다른 모음 없이 혼자 길어지는 경우

be /비-/, me /미-/, she /쉬-/, he /히-/, we /위-/

장모음 e는 e를 하나 더 겹치거나 a와 만나서 ee, ea가 되면 소리가 길어집니다.

ex) bee, see, sea, tea

3) 장모음 I i /아이/

장모음 i와 다른 알파벳을 붙여 소리를 만들어 봅시다.

ide	아이 + 드 ►	ike	아이 + 크 ►
ime	아이 + 음 ► 아임	ine	아이 + 은 ► 아인
ipe	아이 + 프 ► 아잎	ite	아이 + 트 ► 아잍
ive	아이 + 브v ► 아입v		

앞에 여러 가지 자음을 넣어 연습해 봅시다.

ex) ride, bike, time, nine, pipe, kite, five

✔ i 뒤에 오는 c는 /크/가 아니라 /쓰/(soft c)로 발음됩니다.(예 : ice, rice, slice, 등)

4) 장모음 O o /오우/

장모음 o와 다른 알파벳을 붙여 소리를 만들어 봅시다.

obe	오우 + 브 ► 오웁	ole	오우 + 을 ► 오울
ome	오우 + 음 ► 오움	one	오우 + 은 ► 오운
ope	오우 + 프 ► 오욮	ose	오우 + 즈8 ► 오우즈
ote	오우 + 트 ► 오우트		

앞에 여러 가지 자음을 넣어 연습해 봅시다.

ex) robe, hole, dome, cone, rope, rose, note

5) 장모음 U u /유우/

장모음 u와 다른 알파벳을 붙여 소리를 만들어 봅니다.

ube	유우브 ► 윱	uge[9]	유우쥐 ► 유쥐
ule	유우을 ► 율	une	유우은 ► 윤
use	유우즈 ► 유즈	ute	유우트 ► 윹

앞에 여러 가지 자음을 넣어 연습해 봅시다.

ex) cube, tube, huge, mule, June, tune, fuse, cute

【4】 이중자음(Double Consonants)

자음이 서로 만나 소리가 뭉쳐지면(blending) 고유의 소리를 잃고 새로운 소리로 변하는 경우가 있습니다.

c	h	ch /취/
s		sh /쉬/
tc		tch /(읕)취/
t		h /쓰/, /드/
w		wh /워/

새로운 소리로 변하는 이중자음들을 연습해 봅시다.

ex) cherry, shell, match, thank, wheel, when

【5】 이중모음(Double Vowels)

이중모음은 모음 두 개가 나란히 붙어있는 것을 말합니다. 모음이 두 개 겹치면 앞의 모음이 장모음으로 변하면서 뒤의 모음은 소리가 나지 않으며, 각각 고유의 소리 대신 전혀 다른 소리로 바뀌기도 합니다.

---

8 장모음 뒤에 오는 se는 z의 소리값으로 변합니다.

9 단어가 ge로 끝나면 g는 /그/로 소리나지 않고 부드러운 소리로 변합니다.(예 : huge /휴쥐/, page /페이쥐/ 등)

1) —ai, ay /에이/

mail, rain, wait, May, gray, play

2) —ee, ea /이—/

bee, green, pea, leaf

3) —ie /아이/, /이—/

tie/타이/, pie/파이/, piece/피-쓰/, chief/취-프f/

4) —oa, ow /오우/

goat, road, bowl, crow

5) —ui /우-/, —ue /우—/, /유—/

suit, fruit, clue, hue

6) —ar /아얼/, —or /오얼/

car, party, corn, store

7) —ir, er, ur

I		ir /얼/
e	r	er /얼/
u		ur /얼/

bird, skirt, sister, brother, purple, turtle

8) —ou, ow /아우/

mouse, house, cow, down

9) —oi, oy /오이/

boil, toilet, enjoy, oyster

10) —oo /우/, /우—/

book/북/, look/룩/, spoon/스푸-은/, room/루우-음/

Ⅱ. 문장의 기본 구성요소

【1】 품사(Parts of Speech)

성질이 공통된 단어끼리 모아놓은 단어의 갈래를 말하며, 영어에는 8품사가 있습니다.

품사	뜻	예
명사	사람, 사물의 이름	apple, water, John, January
대명사	명사를 대신해서 사용하는 말	I, you, he, she, it, they, this
동사	동작이나 상태	is, am, are, go, walk, love
형용사	성질, 상태, 특징 등을 나타내는 말	small, pretty, good, fast
부사	시간, 장소, 정도, 방법 등을 나타내는 말	now, there, very, much, well
전치사	명사, 대명사 등의 앞에서 도와주는 말	in, on, at, for, to
접속사	앞, 뒤의 말을 연결해서 이어주는 말	and, but, or, when, because
감탄사	기쁨, 슬픔, 놀라움 등	wow, oh, oops

【2】 문자의 4가지 기본적 구성요소

주어(Subject) : 우리말의 '~은/는', '~이/가'에 해당합니다.
동작이나 상태의 주체가 되는 말이며 명사, 대명사가 이 역할을 합니다.

- Today is Wednesday. 오늘은 수요일이다.
- I know Kate. 나는 케이트를 알아.

술어동사(Verb) : '~하다', '~이다'로 쓰이며, 주어의 행동이나 상태를 나타냅니다.

- They are nice. 그것들은 좋다.
- She runs fast. 그녀는 빨리 달린다.

목적어(Object) : '~을/를'에 해당하며, 동사의 행동의 대상이 됩니다.

- I like movies. 나는 영화를 좋아해.
- Lynn plays tennis very well. 린은 테니스를 아주 잘 쳐.

보어(Complement) : 주어나 목적어의 의미를 보충설명하는 말.
주어를 보충설명하는 말은 주격보어, 목적어를 보충설명하는 말은 목적격보어라고 합니다.

- Matt is a great scholar. 매트는 훌륭한 학자야.
- He makes me happy. 그는 나를 행복하게 만든다.

【3】그 외의 문장 구성요소

수식어(구) : 문장의 기본요소를 꾸며주는 말

① 형용사 - 명사(주어, 목적어, 보어)를 꾸며주는 수식어. 우리말의 '~한, ~ㄴ'에 해당합니다.

- Can I have cold water? 찬 물 좀 주시겠어요?
- Jeju is a beautiful island. 제주는 아름다운 섬이다.

② 부사 - 동사(술어동사), 형용사, 다른 부사, 문장 전체를 꾸며주는 수식어. 주로 '-ly'로 끝나는 단어의 형태가 많습니다.

- Please drive carefully. 조심히 운전하세요.
- Unfortunately, she failed to the test. 안타깝게도, 그녀는 시험에 떨어졌다.

구(Phrase) : 둘 이상의 단어가 모여 하나의 의미단위를 이루는 것을 말합니다.

- Come here at once! 당장 이리와!
- To learn a foreign language is difficult. 외국어를 배우는 것은 어렵다.

절(Clause) : [주어 + 동사]가 포함된 덩어리

- Wendy and Steve came here yesterday and they will stay until next week.
  웬디와 스티브는 어제 여기에 왔고 그들은 다음 주까지 머물 것이다.
  ✔ 접속사 and로 연결되는 두 개의 동등한 절
- Amy said that she didn't meet her new boss.
  에이미는 그녀의 새로운 상사를 만나지 못했다고 말했다.
  ✔ 접속사 that으로 주절에 연결되는 명사절

지각동사 / 감각동사 / 사역동사

① 지각동사 : see, hear, notice, feel, watch, look at, listen to 등의 동사

② 감각동사 : feel, sound, taste, look, smell 등 사람의 오감과 관련된 동사

③ 사역동사 : have, let, make, bid, help, get 등과 같이 '~을 시키다'라는 뜻을 지닌 동사

가산명사 / 불가산명사

① 가산명사(Countable noun) : 셀 수 있는 보통명사, 사람이나 사물의 집합체를 나타내는 일반적인 집합명사. 복수일 때는 명사 뒤에 '-s'를 붙이면 됩니다.

예 : a book, books, family, crew, …

② 불가산명사(Uncountable noun) : 셀 수 없이 너무 많거나 형태가 불확실하여 셀 수 없는 명사. 항상 단수로 쓰입니다.

예 : sugar, butter, water, peace, love, information, Korea, …

인칭 : 사람을 가리키는 말

① 1인칭 : 나(I), 우리(we)

② 2인칭 : 너(you), 너희들(you)

③ 3인칭 : 1인칭과 2인칭을 제외한 나머지
그(he), 그녀(she), 그것(it), 그들(they), Jacob 등

Ⅲ. 문장의 형식

영어문장은 크게 다섯 가지의 종류로 이를 영어의 '문장의 5형식'이라고 부릅니다. 문장의 주요 구성요소가 어떻게 결합하느냐에 따라 문장의 형식이 달라지며, 문장의 형식을 이해하면, 영어를 이해하기가 훨씬 쉬워집니다.

형식	형태	예
1	주어(S) + 동사(V)	I work at home.
2	주어(S) + 동사(V) + 주격보어(S.C)	That dress is expensive.
3	주어(S) + 동사(V) + 목적어(O)	I met Chris yesterday.
4	주어(S) + 동사(V) + 간접목적어(I.O) + 직접목적어(D.O)	The manager sent me a letter.
5	주어(S) + 동사(V) + 목적어(O) + 목적격보어(O.C)	Mom keeps her kitchen clean.

1형식

주어와 동사만으로도 완전한 문장이 이루어지며, 1형식 문장의 동사는 목적어나 보어를 필요로 하지 않기 때문에 완전자동사라고 합니다.

- The plane arrived. 비행기가 도착했다.
- The officer walked across the bridge. 경관이 다리를 건너갔다.

✔ 1형식 문장의 구조에 다양한 수식어(구)가 붙으면 문장이 길어질 수 있습니다.

다음 문장을 보고 주어에는 ○, 동사에는 △, 수식어(구)에는 밑줄을 치세요.

1. I live near down town.
2. Ms. Kelly sleeps four hours a day.

2형식

2형식 문장은 1형식 문장에 주격보어가 들어간 문장입니다. 2형식 문장에서의 동사는 주격보어를 필요로 하는 동사로 이를 불완전자동사라고 합니다. 주격보어 자리에는 주로 형용사나 명사(구)가 옵니다.

- My father is a lawyer. 우리 아버지는 변호사야.
- This subject seems difficult. 이 과목은 어려워 보인다.

✔ 대표적인 2형식 동사

상태 : be, keep, remain, stay, lie, stand

변화 : become, get, go, turn out, fall, prove
외견 : seem, appear, look
감각 : sound, feel, taste, smell, look

다음 문장에서 주어에는 ○, 주격보어에는 △를 표시해 보세요.

1. Mathematics is difficult.
2. It sounds interesting.
3. Ms. Park became the president of the Republic of Korea.

3형식

3형식 문장은 1형식 문장에 목적어가 들어간 문장입니다. 3형식 문장의 동사는 목적어를 취하는 동사로 이를 타동사라고 합니다. 목적어 자리에는 명사(구)나 대명사의 목적격이 옵니다.

- We attended the meeting. 우리는 회의에 참석했다.
- The professor announced his plan. 교수님이 계획을 발표했다.

주어진 우리말에 맞게 다음 단어들을 알맞게 배열하세요.

1. 그들은 탐을 매우 사랑한다. ____________________

   (love, Tom, they, very much)
2. 교실은 책상을 40개 갖고 있다. ____________________

   (has, forty desks, the classroom)

4형식

4형식 동사는 목적어를 두 개 취합니다. 간접목적어는 '~에게'에 해당하는 말이고, 직접목적어는 '~을/를'에 해당하는 말입니다.

- He gave Jennifer roses. 그는 제니퍼에게 장미를 주었다.
- They sent us an invitation. 그들은 우리에게 초대장을 보냈다.

✔ 대표적인 4형식 동사

give, send, buy, offer, show, tell, lend, …

✔ 4형식 문장의 3형식으로의 전환

간접목적어와 직접목적어가 들어간 4형식 문장에서, 간접목적어와 직접목적어의 순서를 바꾸고, 간접목적어 앞에 전치사를 붙여서 3형식 문장으로 바꾸어 쓸 수 있습니다.

3형식으로 바뀔 때 함께 쓰이는 전치사

to 를 쓰는 동사	give, send, show, teach, tell, offer
for 를 쓰는 동사	buy, make, get, cook
of 를 쓰는 동사	ask

She offered me some help.(4형식) → She offered some help to me.(3형식)

5형식

5형식 문장은 3형식 문장에 목적격보어가 들어간 구조로 이루어진 문장입니다. 목적격보어에도 형용사나 명사가 오지만, 주격보어와는 다르게 목적어를 보충해 줍니다.

- The police officer found him dead.
  경찰관은 그 남자가 죽었다는 것을 알았다.
- This new project will make our customers happy.
  이 새로운 프로젝트는 우리의 고객들을 기쁘게 할 것이다.

✔ 5형식의 대표적인 동사

make, let, have : ~하게 하다

Too much wine make men drunk.(과음은 사람을 취하게 한다.)

- keep : (어떤 상태/관계에)두다, ~하여두다, 유지하다
  Regular exercise will keep your body healthy.
  규칙적인 운동은 몸을 건강하게 유지한다.
- find : ~라고 생각하다(여기다), ~을 알다, 깨닫다
  Most students found this system very useful.
  대부분의 학생들이 이 시스템을 유용하다고 여긴다.

Ⅳ. 영어의 숫자 표현

【1】 영어의 숫자

기수(Cardinal numbers)라고도 하며, 우리말로 일, 이, 삼, 사, 혹은 하나, 둘, 셋, 넷에 해당하는 숫자들입니다.

【2】 영어의 서수(Ordinal numbers)

서수는 사물의 순서를 나타내는 수입니다.(예 : 첫 번째, 두 번째 등) first, second, third를 제외하면 대부분 기수에 -th를 붙인 형태이며 서수 앞에는 보통 the를 쓰지만, 앞에 소유격이나 this, that 등이 있으면 쓰지 않습니다.
영어에서는 날짜, 층수 등을 말할 때도 서수를 사용합니다.

예) Today is January second. 오늘은 1월 2일이다.
We live on the 6th floor. 우리는 6층에 산다.
Jane was the first in the race. 제인이 경기에서 1등이었어.

	기수	서수	서수 줄임말		기수	서수	서수 줄임말
1	one	first	1st	12	twelve	twelfth	12th
2	two	second	2nd	13	thirteen	thirteenth	13th
3	three	third	3rd	14	fourteen	fourteenth	14th
4	four	fourth	4th	15	fifteen	fifteenth	15th
5	five	fifth	5th	16	sixteen	sixteenth	16th
6	six	sixth	6th	17	seventeen	seventeenth	17th
7	seven	seventh	7th	18	eighteen	eighteenth	18th
8	eight	eighth	8th	19	nineteen	nineteenth	19th
9	nine	ninth	9th	20	twenty	twentieth	20th
10	ten	tenth	10th	21	twenty one	twenty first	21st
11	eleven	eleventh	11th	22	twenty two	twenty second	22nd

	기수	서수	서수 줄임말		기수	서수	서수 줄임말
30	thirty	thirtieth	30th	70	seventy	seventieth	70th
40	forty	fortieth	40th	80	eighty	eightieth	80th
50	fifty	fiftieth	50th	90	ninety	ninetieth	90th
60	sixty	sixtieth	60th	100	hundred	hundredth	100th

【3】 달(월)을 나타내는 영어단어

월(달)	월 영어단어(약자)	월(달)	월 영어단어(약자)
1월	January(Jan)	7월	July(Jul)
2월	February(Feb)	8월	August(Aug)
3월	March(Mar)	9월	September(Sep)
4월	April(Apr)	10월	October(Oct)
5월	May(May)	11월	November(Nov)
6월	June(Jun)	12월	December(Dec)

【4】 요일을 나타내는 영어단어

요일	영어단어(약자)
월요일	Monday(Mon)
화요일	Tuesday(Tue)
수요일	Wednesday(Wed)
목요일	Thursday(Thu)
금요일	Friday(Fri)
토요일	Saturday(Sat)
일요일	Sunday(Sun)

✔ 영어의 달, 요일의 첫 글자는 대문자로 표시합니다.

Let's English

UNIT 1

Hello.

Warm-up

우리말을 보고 영어로 말해 보세요.

1. 안녕하세요?

____

2. 좋은 아침입니다.

____

3. 전 __________ 입니다.

____

4. 성함이 어떻게 되세요?

____

5. 어디 출신이세요?

____

파트너에게 영어로 자신의 이름과 출신을 말해 보세요.

[Example]

A : Hello. My name is Jisu Kim. I'm from Seoul.

B : Hi. My name is David Costner. I'm from New York.

Conversation 1

Track 01 ### *My name is Jisu.*

Mr. Howard	Good morning, class.
	Let me call attendance. Matthew?
Matthew	I'm here.
Mr. Howard	Jisu?
Jisu	I'm here, sir.
Mr. Howard	Oh, are you a new student here, Jisu?
Jisu	Yes, I am. This is my first day at school.
Mr. Howard	Welcome to my class, Jisu.
	Everyone, this is Jisu from South Korea.
	Jisu, can you introduce yourself to the class?
Jisu	Yes, Mr. Howard.
	Hello, everyone, my name is Jisu and nice to meet you all.

New Vocabulary

attendance 출석, 참석　　introduce 소개하다, 도입하다

You Need to Know 1

【1】 be동사의 현재형(Am, are, is)

인칭 \ 수	단 수			복 수		
1인칭	I	나	am	We	우리	are
2인칭	You	너	are	You	너희	
3인칭	He	그	is	They	그(것)들	
	She	그녀				
	It	그것				

✔ be동사의 의미

1. '~이다' : I am 20 years old. 저는 스무 살입니다.
2. '있다' : She is in Busan. 그녀는 부산에 있다.
3. '어떠하다' : John is sick. John이 아프다.

밑줄에 알맞은 be동사를 쓰세요.

1. Mom ______________ in the kitchen. 엄마는 부엌에 계시다.
2. My brother ______________ tall. 내 남동생은 키가 크다.
3. Chris and I ______________ good at math. 크리스와 나는 수학을 잘한다.
4. That dog ______________ cute. 저 개는 귀엽다.
5. Your books ______________ on the desk. 네 책들은 책상 위에 있어.

【2】 be동사 현재형 부정문

주어 + am, are, is + not + ~ : ~이 아니다, ~가 없다

- I am not a student. 저는 학생이 아닙니다.
- My bag is not heavy. 제 가방은 무겁지 않습니다.

※ be동사의 축약형 : be동사는 다음과 같이 줄여서 쓰기도 합니다.

I am = I'm			I am not = I'm not		
You are = You're			You are not = You aren't		
He / She / It	is	= He / She / It 's	He / She / It	Is not	= He / She / It isn't
We / You / They	are	= We / You / They 're	We / You / They	are not	= We / You / They aren't

Check up

다음의 문장을 부정문으로 바꾸어 보세요.

1. She is a cook. ► ______________________
2. They are workers. ► ______________________
3. My sister is angry. ► ______________________
4. This is my book. ► ______________________
5. Your shoes are dirty. ► ______________________

【3】be동사 현재형 의문문

Am, Are, Is + 주어 + ~? : ~은 ~입니까?

- Are you angry? 너 화났니?
- Is it cold outside? 밖이 춥니?

① be동사 문장의 의문문을 만들 때는 주어와 동사의 위치를 바꾸고 마지막에 물음표를 붙입니다.

② 대답은 'Yes, 주어 + be동사.' / 'No, 주어 + be동사 + not.'으로 합니다.

긍정 대답	부정 대답
Yes, I am.	No, I'm not.
Yes, you / we / they are.	No, you / we / they aren't.
Yes, he / she / it is.	No, he / she / it isn't.

다음의 문장을 의문문으로 바꾸어 보세요.

1. She is kind. ► ______________________________?
2. They are at home. ► ______________________________?
3. Will and Dave are busy now. ► ______________________________?

파트너에게 영어로 물어보고, 대답해 보세요.

1. 지금 춥니? ► ______________________________?
2. 너랑 네 선생님은 한국인이니? ► ______________________________?
3. 너희 아버님은 경찰이시니? ► ______________________________?

Conversation 2

Track 02 *Where are you from?*

Steve	Hello. My name is Steve Parker.
Jisu	Hi. I'm Jisu.
Steve	It's nice to meet you, Jisu. What's your last name?
Jisu	It's Kim. Are you from America, Steve?
Steve	Yes, I'm from Boston. Where are you from, Jisu?
Jisu	I'm from Seoul, Korea.
Steve	How is your first day in school?
Jisu	So far so good. Everyone is friendly.
Steve	Good for you!

New Vocabulary

last name(= family name) (이름의) 성

So far so good. 지금까지는 좋다.

exciting 신나는, 재미있는

friendly 친절한

【1】 인칭대명사(Personal Pronouns)

인칭대명사란, 사람(사람들)을 가리키는 대명사입니다. 대화하는 상황에서 1인칭은 나, 2인칭은 너, 3인칭은 나와 너가 아닌 제3자(사람, 동물, 사물)입니다.

인 칭		주 격	소유격	목적격	소유대명사
		~은, ~는, ~이, ~가	~의	~을, ~를, ~에게	~의 것
1인칭	단수	I	my	me	mine
	복수	We	our	us	ours
2인칭	단수	You	your	you	yours
	복수	You	your	you	yours
3인칭	단수	She	her	her	hers
		He	his	him	his
		It	its	it	없음
	복수	They	their	them	theirs

I love Raymond.
We love Raymond.
You love Raymond.
He(She) loves Raymond.
They love Raymond.

Raymond loves me.
Raymond loves us.
Raymond loves you.
Raymond loves him(her).
Raymond loves them.

This is my dog.
This is our dog.
This is your dog.
This is his(her) dog.
This is their dog.

This dog is mine.
This dog is ours.
This dog is yours.
This dog is his.
This dog is theirs.

우리말을 참고하여 밑줄에 알맞은 인칭대명사를 쓰세요.

1. ____________ plays the piano very well. 그는 피아노를 아주 잘 친다.
2. I sent ____________ some flowers. 나는 그녀에게 꽃을 좀 보냈다.
3. The police officer asked ____________ a question. 경찰관이 나에게 질문을 했다.
4. She loves ____________ son very much. 그녀는 아들을 무척 사랑한다.
5. Please give ____________ some food. 우리에게 먹을 것을 좀 주세요.
6. Those books are ____________. 그 책들은 그들의 것이다.
7. Michael hates ____________. 마이클은 널 싫어해.
8. We played with ____________. 우리는 그들과 놀았다.
9. That red car is ____________. 저 빨간 차는 내거야.
10. Tell Tim I miss ____________. 팀에게 내가 보고 싶어한다고 전해줘.

【2】 Wh-의문사

wh-로 시작하는 의문사(who, when, where, what, why, how)를 의문대명사라고 합니다. 의문대명사는 일반적으로 문장 맨 앞에 놓여 의문문을 만들며, be동사와 함께 쓰일 때는 be동사 의문문 앞에 위치합니다.

- **who(누가)**
  Who is the man over there? 저기 있는 남자가 누구니?
- **when(언제)**
  When is your birthday? 네 생일이 언제니?
- **where(어디서)**
  Where is the cell phone? 핸드폰이 어디 있니?

- **what(무엇)**

  What color is your new car? 네 새차가 무슨 색이니?
- **why(왜)**

  Why are you angry? 너 왜 화났어?
- **how(어떻게)**

  How is she? 그녀는 어떻습니까?

✔축약형으로 쓸 수도 있습니다.

Who is = Who's, When is = When's, Where is = Where's,
What is = What's, Why is = Why's, How is = How's

Wh-의문문에 대한 대답을 할 때에는 Yes/No로 대답하지 않습니다.

다음 질문에 알맞은 대답을 찾아보세요.

1. Where is Jack from?	a. Yes, I am	1. ______
2. How are your parents?	b. Traffic jam.	2. ______
3. What is your favorite sport?	c. 19 years old.	3. ______
4. Who is the man in the picture?	d. Vancouver.	4. ______
5. What color is your car?	e. They are fine, thanks.	5. ______
6. Is the game interesting?	f. No, you're not.	6. ______
7. Am I late?	g. Black.	7. ______
8. How old are you?	h. No, it's boring.	8. ______
9. Are you married?	i. He's my dad.	9. ______
10. Why are you late?	j. Swimming.	10. ______

Activity

교실을 돌아다니면서 가능한 많은 친구들의 이름과 전화번호, 이메일 주소, 그리고 출신을 묻고, 표를 완성합니다.

Tips

전화번호를 말할 때, 숫자 0은 zero나 oh로 읽습니다.
이메일 주소에서 @은 at으로, .은 dot으로 읽습니다.

Name ____________________
Phone ____________________
E-mail ____________________
Where from ________________

Name ____________________
Phone ____________________
E-mail ____________________
Where from ________________

Name ____________________
Phone ____________________
E-mail ____________________
Where from ________________

Name ____________________
Phone ____________________
E-mail ____________________
Where from ________________

What's your … ?

파트너에게 궁금한 것들을 물어 보세요.

- What's your name?
- Where are you from?
- How old are you?
- When's your birthday?
- What's your major?
- Who's your best friend?

New Vocabulary

※ major : 전공

여러분이 인터뷰한 파트너를 같은 그룹에 있는 친구들에게 소개합니다.

This is Minho Lee. He's from Daegu and 20 years old.
His birthday is …

파트너와 대화한 내용을 바탕으로 가장 흥미로운 파트너에 대해 아는 것을 써 보세요.

____

____

____

Exercises

A. 다음 질문을 읽고, 대답을 써 보세요.

1. What's your name? ______________________________
2. How old are you? ______________________________
3. Who's your English teacher? ______________________________
4. How are you today? ______________________________
5. How are your parents? ______________________________
6. How is your English class? ______________________________
7. Who are your classmates? ______________________________
8. Pleased to meet you. ______________________________
9. Are you from Japan? ______________________________
10. Is your father a chef? ______________________________

B. 밑줄 친 부분에 맞는 대명사를 쓰세요.

1. They are my friends. __________ names are Will and Pete.
2. Sorry. What's __________ name again?
3. I'm from Jeju. __________ is a beautiful island.
4. I don't eat carrots. I don't like __________
5. Where are my earrings? I can't find __________
6. I need to call Beth. Do you know __________ phone number?
7. Mrs. Jones is very friendly. I like __________
8. Paul needs that book. Can you give __________ to __________?

9. They are going to get married. He loves ______________

10. My parents are on vacation. ______________ are in Europe.

C. 다음의 우리말을 보고 영어 문장을 만들어 보세요.

1. 그들은 키가 큽니다. ______________________________
2. 시험이 어려운가요? ______________________________
3. 그 시험은 쉽지 않아요. ______________________________
4. 어머님이 바쁘시니? ______________________________
5. 저 남자의 이름이 무엇입니까? ______________________________
6. 그는 왜 늦었어요? ______________________________
7. 그들은 어떻게 지내요? ______________________________
8. Mike와 저는 친구입니다. ______________________________
9. 추석은 언제인가요? ______________________________
10. 네가 지혜니? ______________________________

문화 Q&A

영어 이름에는 어떤 뜻이 담겨져 있을까요?

동양의 문화에서는 이름을 지을 때, 뜻을 중요시하는 경우가 많이 있습니다. 뜻뿐 아니라 그 사람의 생일, 태어난 시, 성별 등에 따라 아주 까다롭게 짓기도 하지요. 서양에서는 할머니나 할아버지의 이름을 물려받기도 하고, 유명인이나 유명한 시, 소설 속의 주인공 이름을 따라 짓는 경우도 많습니다. 그러면, 많이 쓰이는 영어 이름의 의미는 어떤지 한 번 살펴볼까요?

남자 이름	뜻	여자 이름	뜻
Aron	하느님의 계시를 받은	Agatha	선량한
Abraham	군중의 아버지	Agnes	정숙한
Adam	남자, 땅	Aileen	빛, 기품 있는, 아름다운
Alan	사냥개, 조화	Alice	기품 있는, 진실
Albert	대단히 뛰어난	Amanda	사랑받을 만한
Alfred	평화, 조언자	Amy	사랑받는
Alexander	조력자	Anna	우아함으로 가득 찬
Andrew	남자다운, 용감한	Angela	천사 같은
Antony	잴 수 없을만큼 큰	Audrey	고결한 힘
Arnold	명예를 중시하는	Beatrice	축복받은, 행복한
Arthur	뛰어난 사람, 곰	Becky	마음을 사로잡는
Benjamin	행운아	Catherine	청순한, 순결한
Charles	남자다운	Cornelia	바다의 보석
Conrad	적절한 조언자	Crystal	깨끗한
Daniel	신을 대신하는 재판관	Dorothy	신이 보낸 선물
David	사랑받는, (성경의)다윗	Elizabeth	신의 숭배자
Donald	용감한 자	Emily	뛰어난
Douglas	짙은 회색	Emma	사랑받는 자
Edgar	행복을 만드는 자	Esther	별, 행운
Edmund	행복을 지키는 자	Florence	꽃이 핀, 아름다운

남자 이름	뜻	여자 이름	뜻
Edward	행복의 옹호자	Gertrude	대단히 정숙한, 사랑받은
Edwin	행복한 정복자	Grace	신의 은혜
Eugene	명문의	Helen	빛, 등불
Frederick	힘센 옹호자	Irene	평화의 여신
Gabriel	신의 힘	Iris	신을 위해 바치다
Geoffrey	신의 평화, 강력한 보호자	Isabelle	정숙
George	농부	Jessica	신이 돌보는
Gilbert	금처럼 빛나는	Jennifer	흰 파도
Gregory	신념이 굳은	Julia	젊은
Herald	용감한 자, 승리자	Lina	빛
Hugh	이상이 높은	Linda	예쁜 사람
Ian	인자한, 자비로운	Lucy	빛
Issac	웃음	Margaret	진주
Jason	치유하는 자	Martha	귀부인
John	신이 준 자	Matilda	기품있는 처녀
Kenneth	온화한 사람	Naomi	나의 기쁨, 유쾌한
Lawrence	월계관을 쓴, 뛰어난 전사	Olivia	요정의 군대
Leonard	사자처럼 힘 센	Pamela	멋진 사람
Leslie	작은 목장	Rachael	(성경)암양
Matthew	신의 선물	Rebecca	약은 여자
Michael	신과 닮은	Sarah	공주
Owen	젊은이	Sophia	영특한 지혜
Patrick	기품있는	Susan	백합
Raymond	힘이 센	Tiffany	신의 모습
Richard	대단히 강한	Valerie	힘
William	평화의 옹호자	Vivian	생생한, 활발한

우리나라에서도 그렇지만, 뜻이 아무리 좋아도 그 시대에 어울리지 않는 느낌이 들면 사람들에게 외면받기도 하지요. 2012년도에 미국에서 가장 인기 있는 아기 이름 베스트 10입니다.

Rank	Male	Female	Rank	Male	Female
1	Lian	Charlotte	6	Caleb	Olivia
2	Noah	Amelia	7	Jackson	Scarlett
3	Aden	Aria	8	Henry	Violet
4	Oliver	Sophia	9	Benjamin	Emma
5	Grayson	Ava	10	Ethan	Lily

Let's English

UNIT

2

How much is it?

여러분의 가방 속 소지품을 꺼내 보고, 그 안에 무엇이 들어있는지 파트너한테 영어로 얘기해 보세요.

What's in your bag?

- ☐ a mirror
- ☐ an mp3 player
- ☐ a wallet
- ☐ an ID card
- ☐ a cell phone
- ☐ an umbrella
- ☐ cosmetics
- ☐ a hairbrush
- ☐ books
- ☐ pens
- ☐ keys

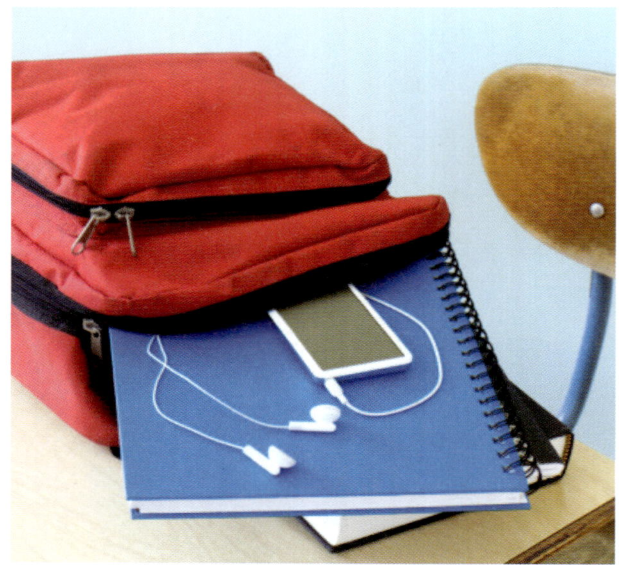

교실에는 무엇이 있는지 영어로 말해 보세요.

What's in our classroom?

- ☐ a board
- ☐ markers
- ☐ a table
- ☐ chairs
- ☐ a wastebasket
- ☐ a map
- ☐ desks
- ☐ pictures
- ☐ a clock
- ☐ a computer
- ☐ an eraser

Conversation 1

Track 03 *How much are they?*

Jisu	Good afternoon.
Clerk	Good afternoon. May I help you?
Jisu	Yes. I'm looking for something for my mom's birthday.
Clerk	Great. Well, these are scarves for ladies. They're made of silk.
Jisu	Hmm… How much is this scarf?
Clerk	It's 90 dollars.
Jisu	Oh, that's too expensive for me. Can you show me those earrings?
Clerk	Sure. Here you are.
Jisu	They are pretty. How much are they?
Clerk	Let me see. They are 35 dollars.
Jisu	Ok. I'll take them.

New Vocabulary

look for ~를 찾다   these/those 이것들/저것들   be made of ~로 만들어진

expensive 비싼   Here you are. (물건 등을 건네줄 때) 여기 있습니다.

You Need to Know 1

【1】 셀 수 있는 명사(가산명사 : Countable nouns)

형태가 구체적으로 있는 사물이나 사람을 가리키는 말

하나일 때 (단수)	단어 앞에 a/an을 붙임	a book, a car, an umbrella
여러 개일 때 (복수)	단어 뒤에 복수형 어미 -s/-es를 붙임	books, cars, dishes

● 명사의 복수형 만드는 법

① 규칙변화

끝이 -x, -z, -s, -sh, -ch	-es	boxes, kisses, benches
끝이 -f, -fe	-ves	wolves, wives, knives
끝이 자음 + o	-es	tomatoes, heroes 예외) pianos, radios
끝이 자음 + y	-ies	babies, candies, countries

② 불규칙변화

a tooth/teeth	a foot/feet	a person/people	a man/men
a child/children	a fish/fish	a sheep/sheep	a deer/deer

③ 항상 복수로 사용하는 명사들

신발류	boots, shoes, sneakers, high heels, slippers, loafers, …
바지류	pants, jeans, shorts, trousers, pajamas
속옷, 양말류	panties, boxers, socks, stockings
안경 및 그 외	contact lenses, glasses, scissors, earrings

✔ people(사람들), police(경찰)도 복수형 명사입니다.

밑줄에 알맞은 명사형을 쓰세요.

1. May I see those __________? 저 손목시계들을 좀 볼 수 있을까요?
2. I wear ____________ 전 안경을 끼어요.
3. Do you have ____________? 남자친구 있으세요?
4. Julia has three ____________ 줄리아는 세 명의 아이가 있어요.
5. Look at the ____________ over there. 저기 있는 사람들 좀 봐.

【2】 셀 수 없는 명사(불가산명사 : Uncountable nouns)

모양이나 형체가 없는 명사. 셀 수 없기 때문에 a/an, -s/-es 등을 붙일 수 없다.

ex) I like orange juice. (O) 나는 오렌지주스를 좋아해.
I like an orange juice. (X)

① 추상명사 : 추상적인 개념 또는 형체가 없는 것

music	weather	love	rain	work	soccer	information
advice	happiness	news	beauty	fun	nature	temperature

- We had fun. 우리는 즐거운 시간을 보냈다.
- Susan loves soccer. 수잔은 축구를 좋아한다.

※ 사건, 예 등을 나타내는 추상명사는 가산명사로 분류됩니다.
ex) idea, suggestion, answer, question, problem, wish 등

- I have an idea. 내게 생각이 있어.

② 물질명사 : 일정한 형태가 없는 액체나 기체, 음식물, 재료

water	coffee	milk	butter	bread	cheese	oil	rice	flour
paper	sugar	soap	grass	hair	clay	cotton	meat	

③ 수의 개념과 어울리지 않는 명사(종합적으로 모인 것)

furniture mail money equipment baggage shopping aircraft

④ 고유명사 : 이름, 국가명, 지명, 브랜드명 등

Korea Monday January James Mt. Everest Lake Tahoe CNN

- Flour is expensive nowadays. 밀가루가 요즘 비싸다.
- I don't drink coffee at night. 전 밤엔 커피를 안 마셔요.

✔ 불가산명사 앞에는 하나를 나타내는 a/an이나 복수형을 쓰지 않습니다. 따라서 많다는 의미의 many를 쓸 수는 없지만, '약간의, 몇몇의'이라는 의미를 지닌 some, 양이 많음을 나타내는 much, 양이 적음을 나타내는 little(거의 없는) (a little : 약간의)은 사용할 수 있습니다.

many는 가산명사와 함께 쓰며, many 다음에는 명사의 복수형이 와야 합니다. 그러나 많다는 의미를 가진 'a lot of, lots of' 다음에는 불가산명사, 복수명사가 모두 올 수 있습니다.

a/an + 단수명사 → an apple, a car, a hat
some + 복수명사 → some cakes, some shoes, some apples
some + 불가산명사 → some money, some milk, some bread
(a) little + 불가산명사 → a little water, little money
much + 불가산명사 → much love, much noise
many + 복수명사 → many schools, many children
a lot of (= lots of) + 복수명사 또는 불가산명사 → a lot of hotels, lots of work

ex) There are many restaurants. 식당들이 많이 있다.
I need some advice. 조언이 필요해.
We had lots of fun. 아주 재밌게 놀았어.
The baby will bring us a lot of happiness. 이 아기가 우리에게 많은 행복을 줄거야.

【3】 단위명사(Unit nouns)

단위를 나타내는 명사를 사용하여 셀 수 없는 대상의 수량을 표현하는 명사.
'수 + 단위 + of + 물질명사'

뜨거운 음료	a cup of two cups of	coffee	다발 / 송이	a bunch of two bunches of	bananas, grapes
찬 음료	a glass of two glasses of	water, milk	통 / 관	a tube of two tubes of	toothpaste
조각	a piece of two pieces of	cake, paper, advice	장	a sheet of two sheets of	paper, glass
얇은 조각	a slice of two slices of	pizza, cheese	캔	a can of two cans of	Coke
긴 병	a bottle of two bottles of	water, shampoo	자루	a bag of two bags of	rice
단지	a jar of two jars of	cream	덩어리	a loaf of two loaves of	bread
파운드 (무게 단위)	a pound of two pounds of	sugar, flour			

다음의 우리말을 영어로 바꾸어 보세요.

1. 피자 두 조각 ► ________________.
2. 주스 세 잔 ► ________________.
3. 치약 세 개 ► ________________.
4. 비누 네 개 ► ________________.
5. 충고 한 마디 ► ________________.
6. 포도 두 송이 ► ________________.

Conversation 2

Track 04 *Which one?*

Jisu	Excuse me. Can you show me that sweater?
Clerk	Which one? This red one?
Jisu	No, the green one over there.
Clerk	This green wool sweater is only 40 dollars.
Jisu	That's not bad. And how much are those sunglasses?
Clerk	Which ones? They are all different.
Jisu	The small black one.
Clerk	They are 135 dollars.
Jisu	May I try them on?

New Vocabulary

which 어느 것, 어느 쪽　　try on 입어 보다

You Need to Know 2

【1】 a/an(부정관사 : Indefinite article)

대화할 때 정해져 있지 않은(부정 : 不定) 일반적인 가산명사 앞에 쓰는 말입니다.

① 가산명사 앞에 쓰며 one(하나)을 뜻할 때

- I saw a cat. 고양이 한 마리를 보았어요.
- Harry is an English teacher. Harry는 영어 선생님이에요.

✔ 모음 발음으로 시작하는 명사 앞에서는 an을 씁니다.

② 종족대표를 나타낼 때

- A dog is a smart animal. 개는 똑똑한 동물이다.

③ a certain(어떤)의 뜻

- A Mr. Brown came to see you. Brown씨라는 분이 널 보러 오셨어.

④ per(마다, 당)의 뜻

- I go to my grandparents' once a week. 난 일주일에 한번씩 조부모님 댁에 가.
- He earns $100,000 a year. 그는 일년에 10만 달러를 번다.

【2】 the(정관사 : Definite article)

상대방도 나도 무엇을 말하는지 확실할 때(정 : 定) 쓰는 말로, 명사 앞에 붙어 지시나 한정을 나타냅니다.

① 앞에 나왔던 명사가 반복될 때

- I bought a cap. The cap is blue. 모자 하나를 샀다. 그 모자는 파란색이다.

② 서로 알고 있는 경우를 가리킬 때

- Can you open the window, please? 창문 좀 열어 주시겠어요?

③ 세상에서 하나 밖에 없는 것을 나타낼 때

- the sun, the moon, the earth, the world, the east, the Pacific, The Amazon, …

④ 기계, 발명품, 악기, 춤 이름 앞에서

- She practices the cello on Saturdays. 그녀는 토요일마다 첼로를 연습한다.
- I listen to the radio a lot. 난 라디오를 많이 들어.

⑤ 최상급, 서수 앞에서

- Tom Cruise is one of the best actors. Tom Cruise는 가장 훌륭한 배우 중 한 사람이다.
- My office is on the sixth floor. 내 사무실은 6층에 있어.

⑥ the same

- We attend the same class. 우린 같은 수업을 들어.

⑦ the top, the end, the middle, the left, …

- I woke up in the middle of the night. 나는 한밤중에 깼다.

잘못된 부분을 바르게 고쳐 보세요.

1. It is a 18 centimeters pen. ______________________
2. There is a books on the shelf. ______________________
3. A bird is in a sky. ______________________
4. Does Stella play a piano well? ______________________
5. I got a F in the exam. ______________________

【3】 관사를 쓰지 않는 경우(무관사)

정관사나 부정관사 등의 한정사 없이 명사가 단독으로 사용되는 경우도 있습니다.

① 총칭적 용도: 구체적인 것이 아니지만 어떤 종류인지 말할 때

- She studies music at college. 그녀는 대학에서 음악을 공부한다.
- We use computers. 우리는 컴퓨터를 사용합니다.(복수명사가 대표명사 역할)

② 계절 및 식사명

- Flowers bloom in spring. 꽃은 봄에 핀다.
- Would you like to go for lunch? 점심 드시러 가실래요?

cf. We had a nice dinner. 우리는 근사한 저녁을 먹었다.

✔ 형용사의 수식을 받을 때는 관사가 옵니다.

③ 운동경기, 놀이

- We played tennis all night. 우리는 밤새 테니스를 쳤다.
- My favorite sport is skiing. 내가 가장 좋아하는 운동은 스키야.

④ 지위, 임무

- Mr. Smith is principal of our school. Smith씨는 우리 학교 교장이다.

⑤ by + 교통, 통신수단

- May goes to school by subway. May는 지하철로 학교에 간다.

✔ 하지만 전치사가 by가 아니면 관사가 있어야 한다.

People are on the bus. 사람들이 버스에 타고 있다.

⑥ 병명

- He battled cancer for many years. 그는 오랫동안 암투병을 했다.
- My father suffers from diabetes. 저희 아버지는 당뇨병으로 고생하고 있어요.

✔ 감기, 통증 등 일부 병명은 관사를 씁니다.

I had a fever. 열이 있어요.

I caught a cold. 감기 걸렸어요.

⑦ church, school, college, bed, home 등의 장소에 본래의 목적으로 가는 경우

- Where did you go to school? 학교는 어디로 다녔니?
- I'm tired. I'm going to bed. 나 피곤해. 자러 갈께.

✔ the bank, the post office, the hospital, the airport, the movies 등에는 the를 씁니다.
I like to go to the movies. 난 영화 보러 가는 것을 좋아해.

⑧ 언어, 거리, 도시, 나라, 공항

- I learned French. 난 프랑스어를 배웠어.
- Namdaemun is in Seoul. 남대문은 서울에 있다.

⑨ TV

- What's on television tonight? 오늘 텔레비전에서 뭐해?

밑줄 친 부분에 알맞은 관사를 넣고, 관사가 필요 없는 경우에는 X 표시를 하세요.

1. Paul usually goes to _______ church every Sunday.
2. We live on _______ same street.
3. _______ sun is shining.
4. He's listening to _______ radio.

Activity

Flea Market

파트너의 물건 중 사고 싶은 것을 골라 가격을 흥정해 보세요. 그룹에서 가장 많은 돈을 번 사람은 누구인가요?

[Example 1]

A : How much is this pen?

B : It's a new pen and it's only 1,000 won.

A : Well, how about 500 won?

[Example 2]

A : What are these?

B : These are leather gloves.

A : How much are they?

A : They are 10,000 won.

B : Oh, they're expensive.

A : They are really nice. Try them on.

자신이 갖고 있는 물건 중에 친구들에게 팔고 싶은 물건들을 골라 가격을 정해 보세요.

[Example]

This is a new notebook.

These are my earrings. They are only 1,000 won.

This beautiful bracelet is only 2,000 won.

These earphones are great. They are 3,000 won.

Exercises

A. 다음 중 알맞은 단어를 골라 문장을 완성하세요.

1. I have (a sister / sister) and two(brother / brothers).
2. Greg gave me (a bread / bread).
3. Do you like (a coffee / coffee)?
4. There are (a woman / women).
5. There is (a salt / salt) on the table.
6. Jeju is (an island / island).
7. I need to buy some (shoe / shoes).
8. I'm going to buy some (a flower / flowers).
9. I don't like (mouse / mice).
10. (A Seoul / Seoul) is the capital of Korea.

B. 다음 중 알맞은 be동사를 골라 문장을 완성하세요.

1. Some people (is / are) always late.
2. Their president (is / are) not popular. The people don't like him.
3. These scissors (is / are) not very sharp.
4. Cheese (is / are) good for bones.
5. Children (is / are) playing on the ground.
6. Many cars (is / are) on the street.
7. Money (is / are) not everything.
8. (Is / Are) this cell phone yours?

9. The Wilsons (is / are) very kind.

10. The police (is / are) looking for a thief.

C. a/an이나 some을 쓰세요.

1. I need ______ money. I want to buy ______ food.

2. Dave has to wear ______ uniform.

3. There is ______ lake in the park.

4. Let me give you ______ advice.

5. Please open the window. We need ______ fresh air.

D. a / an이나 the를 쓰세요.

1. I'm going to London. ______ city has many tourist attractions.

2. "Where is Carol?" "She's in ______ kitchen.

3. Shall we go for ______ walk?

4. It's ______ beautiful day.

5. How was ______ movie?

6. "Oh, It's raining." "Don't worry. I have ______ umbrella."

7. Can you turn off ______ TV?

8. ______ Atlantic is between Africa and the Americas.

9. ______ traffic was terrible this morning.

10. What is ______ name of the street?

E. 아래 보기에서 알맞은 단어를 찾아 쓰세요.(the가 필요한 경우는 함께 씁니다.)

supper	middle	sky	television	time	same	best	airport	floor	summer

1. ______________ is so clear tonight. We can see the stars.
2. We had ______________ late at night.
3. I watched Lee Hyo-ri on ______________.
4. Al and Liz arrived here at ______________ time.
5. Can you tell me ______________?
6. Park Ji-sung is one of ______________ soccer player.
7. Where did you go last ______________?
8. Why are you sitting on ______________?
9. Who is the man in ______________ of the picture?
10. How far is it to ______________?

F. 다음의 우리말을 영어로 영작하세요.

1. 제가 도와드릴까요? ______________________________
2. 남자친구의 생일선물을 찾고 있어요. ______________________________
3. 이 넥타이들은 어떠세요? ______________________________
4. 그것들은 금으로 만들어졌습니다. ______________________________
5. 이 선글라스는 얼마입니까? ______________________________
6. 저 파란 셔츠를 보여주시겠어요? ______________________________
7. 저 구두를 신어볼 수 있을까요? ______________________________
8. 어느 것이 더 좋으세요? ______________________________
9. 저것들은 모두 똑같아요. ______________________________
10. 저쪽에 있는 작은 거요. ______________________________

Yard sale(Garage Sale)

한국에 아나바다가 있다면, 미국에는 Yard Sale(Garage Sale)이 있습니다. 자신에게 필요가 없는 물건들을 자신의 집 앞마당이나 차고에 펼쳐놓고 아주 저렴한 가격에 판매를 하는 것입니다. 주로 이사를 갈 때 짐 정리를 하면서 물건들을 많이 내놓기도 하고, 또 신 학기가 시작되기 전(미국의 경우 7~8월)에도 판매를 많이 합니다. 자신에게 필요가 없어진 물건들을 집 앞마당이나 주차장에 들고 나와 팔게 되는데요, 판매하는 물건은 정말 각양각색입니다. 의류, 책, 장난감, 자질구레한 장식품, 주방용품, 가전제품 외에도 솜씨 좋은 아주머니들은 나와서 쿠키나 케이크를 팔기도 하고, 어린이들은 레모네이드나 시원한 음료를 팔기도 합니다. 종종 희귀하고 진기한 물건을 싼 가격에 구할 수도 있습니다. 미국에서는 이러한 yard sale이 단순히 물건을 사고팔기만 하는 장소가 아닌 지역 주민들의 친목 도모의 장으로도 활용되고 있습니다.

그럼, 사고자 하는 물건값을 흥정할 때 사용하는 표현들을 알아볼까요?

- I like it. But the price is beyond my budget.
  맘에 드는데, 제 예산을 넘네요.
- Can you give me a discount?
  좀 깎아주세요.
- I'll give you some discount.
  제가 좀 깎아드릴께요.

UNIT 3

What do you do?

다음의 직업과 그들이 하는 일을 영어로 말해 보세요.

이미지 출처 : www.tx.english-ch.com

Conversation 1

Track 05 *Do you have a sister?*

Jisu Do you have a sister, Steve?

Steve Yes, I do. She works in a restaurant.

Jisu Oh, really? Which restaurant?

Steve She works in King's Restaurant.

Jisu What does she do?

Steve She's a cook.

Jisu That's wonderful. You can eat nice restaurant food anytime.

Steve Not really. She doesn't cook at home.

Jisu Does she like her job?

Steve I think so. But she doesn't like to cook at home.

New Vocabulary

anytime 언제든지, 언제나 at home 집에서 I think so. 그렇게 생각해

You Need to Know 1

【1】 일반동사 현재형(Verbs : Simple Present)

영어의 현재 시제는 일반적인 사실, 반복적인 행동, 습관, 현재의 상태 등을 나타낼 때 사용합니다.

- I often go to the library after work. 나는 퇴근 후에 자주 도서관에 가.
- The department store opens at 10:30. 그 백화점은 10시 30분에 열어.
- The earth goes around the sun. 지구는 태양 주위를 돈다.

① 주어가 1, 2인칭 단/복수, 3인칭 복수일 때 동사원형(동사의 기본형)을 씁니다.

- They love him. 그들은 그를 사랑해.
- We work in an office. 우리는 사무실에서 일해.

② 주어가 3인칭 단수일 때는 '동사원형 + (e)s'를 씁니다.

- Linda sleeps early. Linda는 일찍 자요.
- George never eats breakfast. George는 아침을 먹지 않아요.

③ 일반동사의 3인칭 단수형 만드는 법

대부분의 동사	+s	reads, loves, drinks, wears, …
자음 + y로 끝나는 동사	y를 i로 고치고 +es	studies, flies, tries, …
모음 + y로 끝나는 동사	+s	plays, enjoys, buys, says, …
s, sh, ch, o, x로 끝나는 동사	+es	washes, goes, does, watches, …
예외동사		have → has

【2】 일반동사 현재형 부정문(Simple Present Negative)

주어 + do (does) not + 동사원형 ~ : ~하지 않다

- I drink coffee. → I don't drink coffee. 나는 커피를 마시지 않는다.
- Bill likes his job. → Bill doesn't like his job. Bill은 그의 일을 좋아하지 않는다.

✔ do not, does not을 줄여서 don't, doesn't로 씁니다.

① 주어가 1, 2인칭 단/복수 및 3인칭 복수일 때 '주어 + don't + 동사원형'

- They don't eat beef. 그들은 소고기를 안먹어.
- You don't know him. 넌 그를 몰라.

② 주어가 3인칭 단수일 때 '주어 + doesn't + 동사원형'

- She doesn't speak Chinese. 그녀는 중국어를 할 줄 몰라.
- This printer doesn't work well. 이 프린터가 잘 작동하지 않아요.

다음을 부정문으로 바꾸어 보세요.

1. I play the piano well. ► ______________________________
2. They know my phone number. ► ______________________________
3. Ted works very hard. ► ______________________________
4. I believe you. ► ______________________________
5. Sue buys a digital camera. ► ______________________________

【3】일반동사 현재형 의문문(Simple Present Questions)

Do/Does + 주어 + 동사원형 ~? ~ 합니까?

- The children like dogs.
  - ► Do the children like dogs? 그 아이들이 개를 좋아하나요?
- He eats fish.
  - ► Does he eat fish? 그는 생선을 먹나요?

① 주어가 1, 2인칭 단/복수 및 3인칭 복수일 때 'Do + 주어 + 동사원형 ~?'

- Do you know him? 너 그를 알아?
  - ► Yes, I do. / No, I don't.
- Do they cook? 그들은 요리를 합니까?
  - ► Yes, they do. / No, they don't.

② 주어가 3인칭 단수일 때 'Does + 주어 + 동사원형 ~?'

- Does your mom have a car? 너네 엄마는 차가 있니?
  - ► Yes, she does. / No, she doesn't
- Does Chen watch TV a lot? Chen은 TV를 많이 보니?
  - ► Yes, he does. / No, he doesn't.

다음을 의문문으로 바꾸어 보세요.

1. You write a letter. ► ______________________________?
2. She cooks dinner. ► ______________________________?
3. They speak English. ► ______________________________?
4. He sings well. ► ______________________________?
5. Carol studies science. ► ______________________________?

Conversation 2

Track 06 *I usually get up early.*

Jisu	Good morning, Jason. How are you?
Jason	Hi, Jisu.
Jisu	Do you jog in the morning?
Jason	Yes, I do. I usually get up early.
Jisu	Really? What time do you get up?
Jason	I get up at five.
Jisu	Wow! That's early. What do you usually do early in the morning?
Jason	I jog, and read a newspaper and some books.
Jisu	You are an early bird! It's difficult for me to get up early.
Jason	Well, it was not easy for me, too. But you'll soon get used to it.

New Vocabulary

usually 보통, 늘
once 일단, 한 번
get up (잠자리에서)일어나다
get used to 익숙해지다
early bird 아침에 일찍 일어나는 사람

You Need to Know 2

【1】 Wh- 현재형 의문문(Simple Present with Wh-questions)

일반동사 현재형 의문문 앞에 wh-의문사를 붙일 수 있습니다.

What do you eat?	너 뭐 먹니?
When do you go to school?	너 언제 학교 가니?
Where does your son live?	당신의 아들은 어디 삽니까?
Who do you like?	넌 누굴 좋아하니?
Why does she leave?	그녀는 왜 떠납니까?
How do you study math?	수학을 어떻게 공부하니?

괄호 안의 단어를 사용하여 의문문을 만들어 보세요.

1. (where / live / your parents) ______________________________?
   당신의 부모님은 어디 사세요?
2. (when / go to bed / you) ______________________________?
   언제 주무세요?
3. (what / this word / mean) ______________________________?
   이 단어가 무슨 뜻이에요?
4. (what / want / you) ______________________________?
   뭘 원하세요?
5. (why / study English / you) ______________________________?
   왜 영어를 공부하세요?

【2】 빈도부사(Adverbs of Frequency)

어떤 일이 얼마나 자주 일어나는지 빈도, 횟수, 정도를 나타내는 부사를 빈도부사라고 합니다.

always	항상, 언제나
usually	보통
often	자주, 종종
sometimes	때때로, 가끔
rarely / seldom	거의 ~않다
never	절대로 ~하지 않다

100%

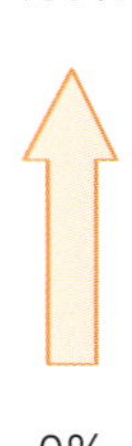

0%

빈도부사의 위치

① be동사, 조동사와 함께 쓰일 때 : be동사/조동사 + 빈도부사

- Carol is always late. Carol은 항상 늦어.
- She will often meet you. 그녀는 너를 종종 만날거야.

② 일반동사와 함께 쓰일 때 : 빈도부사 + 일반동사

- He usually stays up late. 그는 보통 늦게까지 안자고 깨있다.
- You sometimes look unhappy. 너는 때때로 슬퍼 보여.

✔ sometimes는 문장의 앞이나 뒤에 쓰이기도 합니다.

I sometimes eat too much. 나는 때때로 너무 많이 먹는다.

Sometimes I eat too much.

I eat too much sometimes.

괄호 안의 빈도부사를 알맞은 위치에 넣어 문장을 다시 써 보세요.

1. My son calls me.(seldom)

____

2. The dog barks at strangers.(always)

____

3. I can find my wallet.(never)

____

4. Mike wears jeans. (often)

____

5. I will love you.(always)

____

6. What do you do in free time?(usually)

____

7. I am late for school.(rarely)

____

8. Do you eat breakfast?(always)

____

9. He goes to the bar after work.(sometimes)

____

10. I will forget what you said.(never)

____

친구나 가족 중에 한 명을 선택해서 그 사람의 직업에 대해 써 보세요.

【Example】

My sister is a student. She studies hotel management at Daehan college.
She works for a part-time, too. She works at a bar as a server.

____

____

____

파트너에게 질문을 하여, 파트너가 위에서 적은 사람의 직업을 맞추어 보세요.

【Example】

A : Does the person go to school?
B : No, she doesn't.
A : Does she go to work in the morning?
B : No, she starts work in the afternoon.
A : Does she work in a restaurant?
B : Yes, she does.
A : Is she a waitress?
B : No, she isn't.
A : Is she a cook?
B : Yes, she is!

Exercises

A. 다음 중 알맞은 단어를 골라 문장을 완성하세요.

1. Patrick (get / gets) up early.
2. My friends (work / works) hard.
3. Karen (start / starts) work at 9:00 A.M.
4. Evan (speak / speaks) English, Spanish, and Korean.
5. The museum (open / opens) at 10:00 in the morning.
6. My parents (like / likes) to travel.
7. Mark and Tom (study / studies) ancient history.
8. My brother (work / works) in a hospital.
9. Does he (dance / dances) well?
10. Do they (read / reads) newspapers?

B. 아래의 대화문을 알맞은 단어를 골라 완성하세요.

Sue What ___________ (do / does) your wife ___________ (do / does) exactly?

David She ___________ (work / works) for an airline. She's a flight attendant.

Sue How ___________ (do / does) she ___________ (like / likes) it?

David It's an interesting job. She ___________ (like / likes) it very much.

But she ___________ (work / works) long hours. And what ___________ (do / does) you ______ (do / does)?

Sue I'm a student. I ____________ engineering.
(study / studies)

David Oh, really? Where ________ you ____________ to school?
(do / does) (go / goes)

Sue I __________ to Asea College.
(go / goes)

C. 괄호 안의 동사를 이용하여 부정문을 만들어 보세요.

1. I ______________ cleaning my room.(like)
2. I ______________ newspapers very often.(read)
3. Jack ______________ his job very much. He says it's boring.(like)
4. Cara ______________ tea. She likes coffee.(drink)
5. It's not an expensive car. It ______________ a lot.(cost)
6. James is married, but he ______________ a ring.(wear)
7. You ______________ good. Are you alright?(look)
8. My father ______________ me anymore.(believe)
9. Julia ______________ very much. She's a quiet person.(talk)
10. Mark is a vegetarian. He ______________ meat.(eat)

D. 다음 질문에 대한 짧은 본인의 대답을 써 보세요.

1. Do you live with your parents? ______________________________
2. Where do you go to school? ______________________________
3. What do you study? ______________________________
4. How do you like your school? ______________________________
5. Do you have a girl/boy friend? ______________________________

E. 주어진 단어와 빈도부사(always, usually, sometimes, never 등)를 이용하여 자신에 대한 문장을 직접 만들어 봅니다.

【Example】
(watch TV) *I usually watch TV at night.*

1. (hang out with friends) ______________________
2. (go to the movies) ______________________
3. (drink coffee) ______________________
4. (exercise) ______________________
5. (clean up my room) ______________________

F. 다음의 우리말을 영어로 영작하세요.

1. 너 남동생 있니? ______________________
2. 그는 직업이 무엇입니까? ______________________
3. 그는 종종 집에 일찍 오지 않아요. ______________________
4. 우리는 주로 저녁에 공원에서 산책을 합니다. ______________________
5. 내 남자친구는 밤에 늘 컴퓨터 게임을 해. ______________________
6. 난 좀처럼 저녁을 먹지 않아. ______________________
7. 우리 부모님은 주말마다 골프를 치셔. ______________________
8. 그는 나에게 항상 진실을 말해. ______________________
9. Steve는 한국어를 못해. ______________________
10. Ted는 아침에 일찍 일어나지 않아. ______________________

미국에서 인기있는 직업은 무엇인가요?

'직업엔 귀천이 없다'라는 말은 '직업에는 천하고 귀한 것이 없으며 똑같이 중요하다'라는 말입니다. 하지만 살아가다 보면 육체적으로 힘든 일은 하기 싫어하거나 소위 '사'자가 들어가는 직업을 선호하거나 높이 여기는 풍토가 있지요. 이러한 풍토는 우리나라에만 있는 것일까요? 현대 자본주의의 상징, 가장 상업적이고 경제적으로도 활발한 미국의 경우는 어떨까요?

미국의 취업정보전문사이트인 커리어 캐스트(www.careercast.com)가 최근 업무강도, 근무여건, 소득, 스트레스, 취업전망 등 5개 주요 기준에 따라 미국에서 가장 유망한 직업부터 최악의 직업까지 200선을 선정하여 발표하였습니다. 그 중 최고의 직업과 최악의 직업 10선입니다.

Rank	The Best Jobs of 2013	Annual Salary
1	보험계리사(Actuary)	$87,650
2	생의학 엔지니어(Biomedical Engineer)	$81,540
3	소프트웨어 엔지니어(Software Engineer)	$90,530
4	청력검사 기능사(Audiologist)	$66,660
5	금융설계사(Financial Planner)	$64,750
6	치과위생사(Dental Hygienist)	$68,250
7	작업치료사(Occupation Therapist)	$72,320
8	검안사(Optometrist)	$94,490
9	물리치료사(Physical Therapist)	$76,310
10	컴퓨터시스템 분석가(Computer System Analyst)	$77,740

Rank	The Worst Jobs of 2013	Annual Salary
1	신문기자(Newspaper Reporter)	$36,000
2	벌목공(Lumberjack)	$32,870
3	직업군인(Enlisted Military Personnel)	$41,998
4	배우(Actor)	$17.44/hour
5	석유굴착 노동자(Oil Rig Worker)	$37,640
6	낙농업자(Dairy Farmer)	$60,750
7	계량기 검침원(Meter Reader)	$36,400
8	집배원(Mail Carrier)	$53,090
9	지붕 수리공(Roofer)	$34,220
10	항공기 승무원(Flight Attendant)	$37,740

한국에선 들어보지 못한 생소한 직업들도 많이 있습니다. 또한 한국에서는 인기가 많아 취업하기 힘든 직종의 직업들이 미국에서는 그다지 선호하는 직업군이 아님을 볼 수 있습니다. 미국사회 역시 인구의 고령화, 노령화 영향으로 의료분야의 직업군들이 유망 직업군으로 많이 나타나고 있습니다.

자신이 좋아하는 일을 하는 것이 본인에게는 최고의 직업이겠지만, 진로를 고민하는 사람들에게 이 지표는 참고가 될 수 있을 듯합니다. 미국의 직업 전문가들은 "당장의 인기있는 직업이나 학과보다는 사회의 변화의 흐름을 읽으라."고 주문합니다. 전문가들은 이 밖에도 "자신이 활발하게 활동할 30~40대의 적령기에 유망한 직업을 미리 고려해 직업과 관련한 미래를 준비하라."고 말합니다.

구직활동을 하면서 필요한 영어 표현들을 살펴볼까요?

- I'm looking for a job. 직장을 구하고 있어요.
- I'm between jobs. 취업 준비중이에요.(실직상태에요.)
- I worked as a hair dresser. 전 미용사로 일했어요.
- I'm working part-time. 전 아르바이트를 합니다.
  = I have a part-time job.

UNIT

4

Did you have a good time?

지난 방학 때 한 일들을 골라 보세요.

- ☐ read
- ☐ travel
- ☐ shopping
- ☐ go to a museum
- ☐ go camping
- ☐ swim
- ☐ study English
- ☐ watching movies
- ☐ come home late
- ☐ go on a picnic
- ☐ do a part-time
- ☐ visit family
- ☐ get a license
- ☐ play computer games
- ☐ have fun
- ☐ meet with friends
- ☐ exercise
- ☐ take a test
- ☐ help parents
- ☐ play sports

친구들에게 지난 방학 때 한 일들을 영어로 말해 보세요.

【Example】
I met my old school friends. We talked a lot. We had a great time.

Conversation 1

Track 07 *Did you have a good weekend?*

Jisu	Hi, Steve. Did you have a good weekend?
Steve	Well, I had a busy weekend.
Jisu	Oh, what did you do?
Steve	I met an old friend of mine from New York and worked part-time. Then I went grocery shopping for this week.
Jisu	Wow! You must be very tired.
Steve	I am. How about you? What did you do on the weekend?
Jisu	I stayed home and studied for today's test.
Steve	What? Do we have a test today? I didn't know that.
Jisu	Don't worry. You'll pass.

New Vocabulary

a friend of mine 내 친구 하나   grocery 식품, 잡화   pass 통과하다, 합격하다

You Need to Know 1

【1】 일반동사 과거형(Verbs : Simple Past)

영어의 과거시제는 현재와 관련이 없는 과거 사실을 나타낼 때 사용하며, '~ 했다'를 의미합니다. 주로 동사의 기본형에 -ed를 붙여 만들며, 과거시제를 나타내는 부사(ago, yesterday, last night, …) 등과 함께 쓰입니다.

① 규칙 동사형

대부분의 동사	+ed	called, visited, talked, played
e로 끝나는 동사	+d	liked, lived, closed, loved
자음 + y	y를 i로 고치고 +ed	studied, cried, tried, carried
단모음 + 단자음으로 끝나는 동사	마지막 자음 하나 더 쓰고 +ed	stopped, dropped, hopped
2음절 단어에서 뒤에 강세가 오는 동사	마지막 자음 하나 더 쓰고 +ed	admitted, controlled

- My grandfather passed away last year. 우리 할아버지는 작년에 돌아가셨어.
- He studied so hard to enter the university. 그는 그 대학에 가려고 열심히 공부했다.

② 불규칙 동사형

begin - began	build - built	have - had	go - went
drink - drank	do - did	see - saw	give - gave
tell - told	write - wrote	meet - met	buy - bought

- He came back from Japan last night. 그는 어젯밤 일본에서 돌아왔다.
- I lost my wallet the other day. 나는 며칠 전에 지갑을 잃어버렸다.

③ 현재형과 과거형의 모양이 같은 동사

hit - hit	put - put	cut - cut	hurt - hurt
cost - cost	set - set	shut - shut	let - let
quit - quit	fit - fit	split - split	※ read - read [ri:d] - [red]

✔ read의 과거형은 발음에 주의

【2】 일반동사 과거형 부정문(Simple Past Negative)

주어 + did not (didn't) + 동사원형 ~ : ~하지 않았다

인칭에 관계없이 '주어 + did not(didn't) + 동사원형'을 씁니다.

- I called you this morning.
  - ► I didn't call you this morning. 오늘 아침에 전화하지 않았다.
- Carol worked yesterday.
  - ► Carol didn't work yesterday. Carol은 어제 일을 하지 않았다.
- They had dinner together.
  - ► They didn't have dinner together. 그들은 함께 저녁을 먹지 않았다.

다음을 부정문으로 바꾸어 보세요.

1. Jeff did his homework. ► ______________________
2. The Korean team won. ► ______________________
3. You visited here a month ago. ► ______________________
4. They watched the soccer game. ► ______________________
5. I went out for shopping yesterday. ► ______________________

【3】 일반동사 과거형 의문문(Simple Past Questions)

Did + 주어 + 동사원형 ~? ~했습니까?

- You bought a new book.
  - ► Did you buy a new book? 너 새책을 샀니?
- He read a lot of books.
  - ► Did he read a lot of books? 그는 책을 많이 읽었습니까?

인칭에 관계없이 'Did + 주어 + 동사원형 ~?'을 쓰고, 대답은 'Yes, 주어 + did.' / 'No, 주어 + didn't.'로 합니다.

- Did you wash your hands? 너 손 씻었니?
  - ► Yes, I did. / No, I didn't.
- Did your mom make this cake? 어머니께서 이 케이크를 만드셨니?
  - ► Yes, she did. / No, she didn't.

다음을 의문문으로 바꾸어 보세요.

1. You played the piano. ► ______________________?
2. Mr. Smith taught geography last year. ► ______________________?
3. He liked it. ► ______________________?
4. She met her boyfriend. ► ______________________?
5. It rained a lot yesterday. ► ______________________?

【4】 Wh- 과거형 의문문(Simple Past with Wh- Questions)

일반동사 과거형 의문문 앞에 wh-의문사를 붙일 수 있습니다.

What did you study?	너 뭘 공부했니?
When did you wake up?	너 언제 일어났니?
Where did she live?	그녀는 어디 살았습니까?
Who did you see?	넌 누굴 봤니?
Why did they do that?	그들은 왜 그걸 했습니까?
How did you get there?	거기 어떻게 갔습니까?

괄호 안의 단어를 사용하여 의문문을 만들어 보세요.

1. (who / like the most / he) ______________________?
   그는 누굴 가장 좋아했어요?
2. (where / get that / you) ______________________?
   어디서 그것을 구하셨나요?
3. (what / say / you) ______________________?
   뭐라고 말했어요?
4. (when / arrive / Ms. Jones) ______________________?
   Jones씨가 언제 도착하셨나요?
5. (how / find me / they) ______________________?
   그들이 어떻게 저를 찾았지요?

Conversation 2

Track 08 *I was born in Santiago.*

Jisu Where were you born, Antonio?
Antonio I was born in Santiago.
Jisu Santiago, Chile? How nice!
Antonio You're right.
It's a beautiful city with many historic buildings.
Jisu How wonderful! I want to go there someday.
When did you come to America?
Antonio I came here in 2005.
Jisu You were pretty young, then.
Antonio Yeah, I was only fifteen.
Jisu Did you come here with your family?
Antonio No, I came here alone.
My parents are in Santiago.

New Vocabulary

historic 역사적인 someday 언젠가, 머지않아 pretty 꽤 then 그때는

You Need to Know 2

【1】 be동사의 과거형(Was, were)

수 / 인칭	단수			복수		
1인칭	I	나	was	We	우리	were
2인칭	You	너	were			
3인칭	He	그	was	They	그(것)들	
	She	그녀				
	It	그것				

'~이었다', '있었다'의 뜻으로 쓰입니다.

- I was in San Francisco last year. 나는 작년에 샌프란시스코에 있었다.
- The weather was nice yesterday. 어제 날씨는 좋았다.
- We were very tired. 우린 너무 피곤했다.

【2】 be동사 과거형 부정문

주어 + was, were + not + ~ : ~이 아니었다, ~가 없었다

be동사 과거형 뒤에 not만 붙이면 되며, 축약형으로도 쓸 수 있습니다.

- He was not(wasn't) very busy. 그는 바쁘지 않았다.
- We were not(weren't) at the airport. 우리는 공항에 있지 않았다.

✔ 과거를 나타내는 부사구

yesterday : 어제	last year : 작년	yesterday morning : 어제 아침
two days ago : 2일 전에	last night : 어젯밤	three weeks ago : 3주 전에
last week : 지난 주	two months ago : 2달 전에	last month : 지난 달
three years ago : 3년 전에	then : 그 때	at that time : 당시에, 그 때

다음의 문장을 부정문으로 바꾸어 보세요.

1. You were sad then. ► ____________________
2. Gary was at the party last night. ► ____________________
3. Bill was on vacation last week. ► ____________________
4. They were kind to her. ► ____________________
5. I was very hungry. ► ____________________

【3】 be동사 과거형 의문문

Was, Were + 주어 + ~? : ~은 ~이었니?

- Were you a student? 너는 학생이었니?
- Was he happy? 그는 행복했니?

긍정 대답	부정 대답
Yes, I was.	No, I was not(= wasn't).
Yes, you/we/they/ were.	No, you/we/they were not(= weren't).
Yes, he/she/it was.	No, he/she/it was not(= wasn't).

다음의 문장을 의문문으로 바꾸어 보세요.

1. You were afraid of dogs. ► ____________________?
2. He was tired after the trip. ► ____________________?
3. Jake was in bed at 10:00. ► ____________________?

【4】 Wh- be동사 과거형 의문문(Past be-verb with Wh- Questions)

be동사 과거형 의문문 앞에 wh-의문사를 붙일 수 있습니다.

Who was your homeroom teacher?	누가 네 담임선생님이었니?
When was your anniversary?	네 기념일이 언제였니?
Where were the keys?	열쇠가 어디에 있었니?
What was your favorite subject?	가장 좋아하는 과목이 뭐였니?
Why were you so angry?	너 왜 그렇게 화났었어?
How were they?	그들은 어떠했습니까?

다음의 우리말을 영어로 바꾸어 보세요.

1. 왜 슬펐니? ► ____________________?
2. 그녀는 누구였니? ► ____________________?
3. 너 어젯밤 어디 있었니? ► ____________________?

지난 주말에 했던 일 다섯 가지와 하지 않았던 일 다섯 가지를 적어 보세요.

Things I did	Things I didn't do

파트너에게 자신의 주말 이야기를 해 보세요.

【Example】

A : I watched a movie last weekend.

B : Oh, what was it?

A : It was "Lincoln".

B : I didn't see a movie. But I watched TV.

...

여행지에서 친구에게 엽서를 써 보세요. 다 쓰고 난 뒤 조원들과 함께 엽서를 바꾸어서 읽어 봅니다.

Dear Jesse,

I'm having a great time. I came here with my family yesterday and we went on a tour of the city. I went shopping with my mom and bought some nice accessories. We tried authentic Thai food, too. See you in Seoul. Take care.

Love,

Minhee

Exercises

A. 다음 동사의 과거형을 쓰세요.

1. invite ________	2. become ________	3. keep ________
4. wear ________	5. work ________	6. write ________
7. show ________	8. ring ________	9. grow ________
10. look ________	11. forgive ________	12. draw ________
13. wait ________	14. win ________	15. know ________

B. was, were, wasn't, weren't 중에 알맞은 말을 골라 완성하세요.

Sue How ________ your vacation, David?

David It ________ great! I ________ in New York.

Sue How long ________ you there?

David We ________ there for a week.

Sue ________ you in New York all the time?

David No, we ________. We went to Boston for a day.

Sue And how ________ the weather? ________ it good?

David No, it ________ very good. The city ________ very hot.

C. 괄호 안의 동사를 이용하여 아래의 대화를 완성해 보세요.

Jane We ________ a great time at June's birthday party last night.(have)

Jeff Right. Did you and Kate also ________ it?(enjoy)

Greg No, we didn't. We ________ a boring time.(have)

Jane Why didn't you __________ fun?(have)

Greg We didn't __________ many of the people there.(know)

So we didn't __________ to anyone.(talk)

Jeff That's too bad.

Why didn't you __________ and __________ us?(come / join)

Greg You __________ so happy to see your old friends.(look)

Jane Oh, don't worry, Greg.

I'll introduce my friends to you next time.

D. 다음 질문에 대한 짧은 본인의 대답을 써 보세요.

1. Did you have breakfast this morning? ____________________
2. Where did you go for your vacation? ____________________
3. What time did you wake up today? ____________________
4. How did you come to school? ____________________
5. Did you finish your homework? ____________________

E. 다음의 우리말을 영어로 영작하세요.

1. 무엇을 했습니까? ____________________
2. 주말은 잘 보냈어요? ____________________
3. 피곤하시겠어요. ____________________
4. 언제 태어나셨어요? ____________________
5. 언제 한국에 오셨나요? ____________________
6. 여기에 가족과 함께 오셨나요? ____________________
7. 우리는 좋은 시간을 가졌습니다. ____________________
8. 우리는 저녁으로 비빔밥을 먹었어. ____________________
9. 지난 주말에 비가 왔어. ____________________

문화 Q&A

왜 영어가 세계 공용어가 되었을까요?

살아가면서 과연 한국사람들처럼 영어 때문에 스트레스를 받는 국민들이 또 있을까요? 여러분은 왜 영어를 공부하세요? 우리가 영어 공부를 그렇게 열심히 하는 것은 아마도 세계 공용어로 활용될 정도로 널리 쓰이는 영어를 구사해야 남보다 앞서 나가고, 취업도 잘되고, 해외여행을 가서 의사소통도 되는 등등의 이유가 아닐까 싶습니다.

그렇다면 영어는 어떻게 세계 공용어로서의 위치를 갖게 되었을까요?

먼저, 세계 최강대국인 미국의 언어가 영어인 것도 한 몫 하겠지만, 과거 영국이 전세계 식민지 정복을 하면서 그 지배를 받던 국가들이 자연스레 영어를 사용하게 되면서 영어가 그 나라의 국어 또는 공용어가 된 것이 큰 이유입니다. 영국은 빅토리아 여왕 시대(재위 1837~1901)에 "해가 지지 않는 나라"라는 칭송을 받을 정도로 역사상 가장 많은 영토를 확보하고 가장 화려한 전성기를 누렸습니다. 과거 영국의 식민지였던 나라는 미국, 캐나다, 호주, 뉴질랜드, 인도, 홍콩, 싱가포르, 말레이시아, 가나, 나이지리아, 케냐, 자메이카, 등 전세계에 걸쳐 60여 개가 넘었습니다.

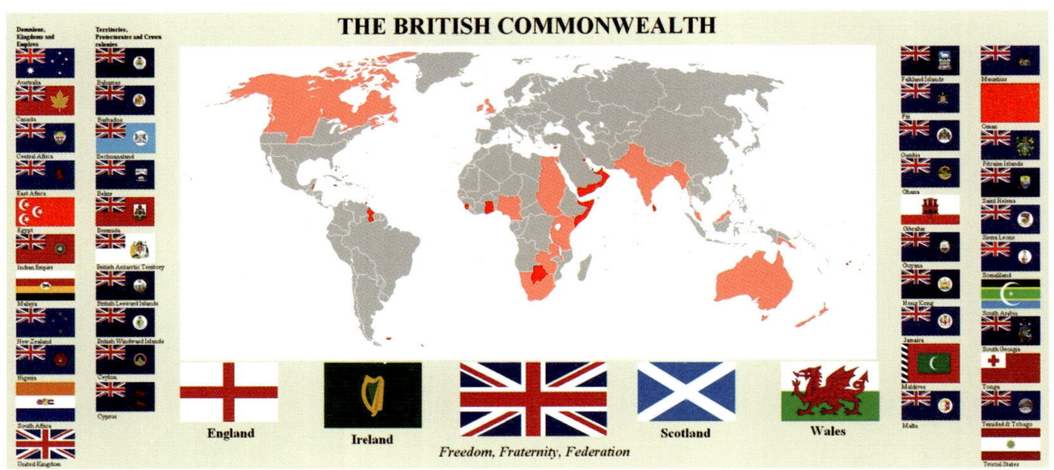

이들 국가 중 52개 국가들은 현재 영국연방(British Commonwealth)에 가입하여 영국을 중심으로 경제, 문화, 교육, 스포츠, 자선 등에 걸친 수많은 협력사업을 추진하고 있습니다. 영연방 회원국들의 인구를 모두 합치면 20억이 넘고 회원국들의 면적을 모두 합치면 지구 면적의 21%를 차지합니다.

현재 영어를 사용하는 나라는 어디일까요?

영어를 법률상 공식언어로 사용하는 나라(55개국)	영어가 사실상의 언어로 사용되고 있는 나라(6개국)	비독립체 국가로서 영어를 사용하고 있는 나라(28개국)
캐나다, 인도, 피지, 아일랜드, 자메이카, 말라위, 몰타, 나이지리아, 피키스탄, 필리핀, 싱가포르, 남아프리카, 파푸아뉴기니, 솔로몬 제도, 등	영국, 호주, 뉴질랜드, 미국 등	버뮤다, 브리티쉬 버진 아일랜드, 괌, 홍콩, 푸에르토리코, 쿡 제도, 등

멸종위기 동물들처럼 세계의 어떤 언어들은 멸종되고 있다고 합니다. 세계화의 흐름에 발맞추려면 영어권 나라가 아니더라도 기본적으로 영어로 의사소통하는데 문제가 없어야 하겠지만, 우리의 자랑스런 문화유산인 국어와 한글을 올바르게 공부하고 사용, 보전하는 것 역시 중요한 일이겠지요.

UNIT 5

What are you doing?

Warm-up

사진을 보고, 무엇을 하고 있는 중인지 말해 보세요.

1.

2.

3.

4.

5.

6.

Conversation 1

Track 09  *What are you doing?*

Steve calls Jisu on the phone.

Jisu Hello.

Steve Hi, Jisu. It's Steve. What are you doing?

Jisu Oh, hi, Steve. I'm reading.

Steve What are you reading?

Jisu Well, I'm reading a book for my homework.

Steve Oh? What's your homework?

Jisu I have to write an essay for English class.
What about you? What are you doing?

Steve I'm having coffee with Marcos.
Do you want to join us?

Jisu Ok. I'll be there by three.

New Vocabulary

homework 숙제 essay 에세이 class 수업, 클래스 join (기다리고 있는 사람과)만나다, 합류하다

You Need to Know 1

【1】 현재진행형

주어 + be동사 현재 + 동사원형-ing : ~하고 있다

- We are reading books. 우리는 책을 읽고 있다.
- Jason is playing soccer. 제이슨은 축구를 하고 있다.

동사원형-ing 만드는 법

대부분의 동사	+ing	go-going / look-looking
-e로 끝나는 동사	-e를 없애고 ing를 붙인다.	come-coming / make-making
단모음 + 단자음	마지막 자음 하나 더 붙이고 +ing	stop-stopping / cut-cutting
-ie로 끝나는 동사	ie를 y로 바꾸고 +ing	lie-lying / die-dying

✔ have, love, like, know 등 상태, 동작, 감정 동사는 현재진행형으로 쓸 수 없습니다.
예) I am loving her.(X) ► I love her.(O)

단, have가 '먹다'라는 뜻으로 쓰일 때는 진행형을 쓸 수 있습니다.
예) Mom is having her breakfast. 어머니가 아침을 먹는 중이다.

Check up

다음을 우리말에 맞게 영어로 쓰시오.

1. 그녀는 편지를 쓰고 있다. ► She ____________ a letter.
2. 존과 메리는 TV를 보고 있다. ► John and Mary ____________ TV.
3. 그는 모자를 쓰고 있다. ► He ____________ a cap.

【2】 현재진행형 부정문

주어 + be동사 현재 + not + 동사원형-ing : ~하고 있지 않다

- Tom is not running. 탐은 뛰고 있지 않다.
- They are not dancing. 그들은 춤추고 있지 않다.

다음을 우리말에 맞게 영어로 쓰시오.

1. 그는 그의 방을 청소하고 있지 않다. ► He ______________ his room.
2. 나는 음악을 듣고 있지 않다. ► I ______________ to music.
3. 그들은 리즈와 얘기하고 있지 않다. ► They ______________ to Liz.

【3】 현재진행형 의문문

be동사 현재 + 주어 + 동사원형-ing? : ~하고 있습니까?

- They are eating lunch.
  ► Are they eating lunch? 그들은 점심식사를 하고 있습니까?
- The baby is sleeping in the room.
  ► Is the baby sleeping in the room? 아기가 방에서 자고 있습니까?

대답은 Yes, 주어 + be동사 현재. / No, 주어 + be동사 현재 + not.으로 합니다.

- Are you going to the grocery store? 당신은 수퍼로 가고 있습니까?
  ► Yes, I am. / No, I'm not.(I'm = I am)

- Is he swimming? 그는 수영을 하고 있습니까?
  - ► Yes, he is. / No, he isn't.(isn't = is not)

✔ 현재진행형은 현재 진행 중인 동작을 나타냅니다.
예) I am working.(현재 일하고 있는 중)

현재형은 현재의 사실이나 습관, 일반적인 진리 등을 나타냅니다.
예) He works at office.(현재 사무실에서 일한다는 사실)

다음을 우리말에 맞게 영어로 쓰시오.

1. 그는 지금 여기 오고 있니? ► ________ he ________________ here?
2. 너는 지금 그거 얘기하고 있는 거야? ► ________ you ________________ about it?
3. 그들은 영어 공부하고 있는 거야? ► ________ they ________________ English?

【4】 Wh- 현재진행형 의문문

What + be동사 현재 + 주어 + 동사원형-ing? : 무엇을 ~하고 있습니까?

- What are you doing? 너 뭘하고 있니?
- Who are you waiting for? 누구를 기다리고 있어?
- When is David coming? 데이빗은 언제 오니?

✔ 현재 진행형은 가까운 미래시제를 나타내기도 합니다. 주로 '왕래발착'(go, come, leave, arrive) 동사들은 현재 진행형으로 예정된 미래를 나타낼 수 있습니다.
ex) When is the plane coming? 비행기가 언제 도착하니?
It's arriving at 3 o'clock. 세 시에 도착할 예정이야.

다음을 우리말에 맞게 영어로 쓰시오.

1. 어디 가는 중이야? ► ____________ you ____________?
2. 몇 시에 돌아오세요? ► ____________ you ____________ back?
3. 누구한테 이메일 보내세요? ► ____________ you ____________?

【5】 현재진행형 vs. 현재형

현재진행형은 화자가 말을 하고 있는 바로 그 시점에 대한 표현이고, 일반동사의 현재형은 늘, 대게, 또는 때때로 일어나는 일에 대한 표현입니다.

ex) A : Where's Tom? Tom 어디 있니?
B : He's taking a shower. (지금)샤워하고 있는 중이야.

A : How's the weather in summer? 여름 날씨는 어떠한가요?
B : it rains a lot. 비가 많이 옵니다.

✔ 진행형으로 쓸 수 없는 동사 : 존재, 상태, 소유의 의미를 갖고 있는 동사들은 진행형으로 사용하지 않습니다.
존재 - be, exist, belong
상태 - know, remember, understand, imagine
감정 - like, love, hate, feel, prefer, want, wish, see, smell, hear, taste
소유 - have, belong to, contain, own, possess

Conversation 2

Track 10 *You shouldn't miss Pacific Park.*

Marcos Hey, Jisu. It's good to see you.
Jisu Hello, Marcos. How are you?
Marcos Pretty good.
I heard you were doing your homework.
Jisu Right. I have to read a book for my essay.
I'm pretty busy nowadays.
How about you, Marcos? What were you doing?
Marcos Oh, Steve and I were discussing about our trip to Santa Monica.
Steve Yeh, do you have any idea what places we should go?
Jisu You shouldn't miss Pacific Park.
It's my favorite place to visit.
It's an amusement park with lots of attractions.
Steve It sounds great!

New Vocabulary

nowadays 요즘　miss 놓치다　amusement park 놀이공원　attraction 어트랙션(놀이기구), 매력

You Need to Know 2

【1】 과거진행형

주어 + be동사 과거 + 동사원형-ing : ~하고 있었다

- I was talking to mom. 엄마랑 얘기하고 있었어.
- We were taking an exam. 우리는 시험을 보고 있었어.

다음을 우리말에 맞게 영어로 쓰시오.

1. 나는 체육관에 가는 중이었어.

   ► I ______ __________ to the gym.

2. 강아지와 산책 중이었어.

   ► I ______ __________ a walk with my dog.

3. Brian과 Tom은 장을 보고 있었어.

   ► Brian and Tom ______ __________ at the supermarket.

【2】 과거진행형 부정문

주어 + be동사 과거 + not + 동사원형-ing : ~하고 있지 않았다

- I was not watching TV. 나는 TV를 보고 있지 않았다.
- They were not working. 그들은 일하고 있지 않았다.

✔ be동사 과거 + not을 축약형으로 쓸 수 있습니다.
예) was not = wasn't　　were not = weren't

Check up

다음을 부정문으로 바꾸어 보시오.

1. They were reading books. ► They ______________ books.
2. I was waiting for Tom. ► I ______________ for Tom.
3. She was dancing in the hall. ► She ______________ in the hall.

【3】 과거진행형 의문문

be동사 과거 + 주어 + 동사원형-ing? : ~하고 있었습니까?

대답은 Yes, 주어 + be동사 과거. / No, 주어 + be동사 과거 + not.으로 합니다.

- Were you going to the grocery store? 당신은 수퍼로 가고 있습니까?
  ► Yes, I was. / No, I wasn't.(wasn't = was not)
- Was he swimming? 그는 수영을 하고 있습니까?
  ► Yes, he was. / No, he wasn't.(wasn't = was not)

다음을 우리말에 맞게 영어로 쓰시오.

1. 10:30에 무엇을 하고 있던 중이었나요? ► What ________ you ________ at 10:30?
2. 너 집으로 운전 중이었어? ► ________ you ________ home?
3. 그는 테니스를 치고 있던 중이었니? ► ________ he ________ tennis?

시간을 나타내는 영어표현을 알아봅시다.

It's three o'clock

It's three-oh-five.
It's five after three.

It's three-fifteen.
It's a quarter after three.

It's three-thirty.
It's half past three.

It's three-forty.
It's twenty to four.

It's three forty-five.
It's a quarter to four.

오전 : It's seven (o'clock) in the morning. = It's 7:00 A.M.
정오 : it's twelve (o'clock). = It's 12:00 P.M. = It's noon.
오후 : It's two (o'clock) in the afternoon. = It's 2:00 P.M.
저녁 : It's six (o'clock) in the evening. = It's 6:00 P.M.
밤 : It's ten (o'clock) at night. = It's 10:00 P.M.
자정 : it's twelve (o'clock) at night. = It's 12:00 A.M. = It's midnight.

Activity

파트너에게 핸드폰으로 전화를 걸어 지금 뭐하고 있는 중인지 묻고 대답해 보세요.

【Example】

A : Hi, Leslie. What are you doing?

B : Hey, Kelly. I'm surfing the web.

A : Oh, Is there anything interesting on the internet?

B : No, I'm just checking my emails and Facebook.

Exercises

A. 다음의 문장을 부정문과 의문문 문장으로 바꾸어 보세요.

1. They are studying English.
- 부정문 : ________________________________
- 의문문 : ________________________________?

2. Chris was driving his car.
- 부정문 : ________________________________
- 의문문 : ________________________________?

3. The boys are running fast.
- 부정문 : ________________________________
- 의문문 : ________________________________?

4. Jacob was working at the office.
- 부정문 : ________________________________
- 의문문 : ________________________________?

B. 빈 칸에 am / is / are 또는 do / don't / does / doesn't를 쓰세요.

1. Excuse me, __________ you speak English?
2. A : Who is she?

   B : I __________ know.
3. It __________ raining. I __________ want to go out.
4. Why __________ you laughing?
5. Pam is a good tennis player, but she__________ play very often.

C. 빈 칸에 과거 진행형 또는 과거형 동사를 쓰세요.

1. A : What __________ (you/do) when the phone __________ (ring)?
   B : I __________ (have) dinner.
2. We __________ (meet) at the gym while I __________ (run).
3. I __________ (drive) home when she __________ (call) me.
4. A : Was Tina at school today?
   B : No, she __________ (not/go) to school. She was sick.
5. A : How __________ (you/break) the window?
   B : We __________ (play) baseball. I __________ (hit) the ball.

D. 다음의 우리말을 참고하여 영어로 말해 보세요.

1. 뭘 읽고 있니? ______________________________
2. 영어 숙제를 해야만 해. ______________________________
3. 세 시까진 갈께. ______________________________
4. 숙제하고 있는 중이라고 들었어. ______________________________
5. 요즘 꽤 바빠. ______________________________

E. 어제 오후에 무엇을 하고 있었는지 과거진행형을 사용하여 영어로 말해 보세요.

【Example】
I was meeting with friends at Starbucks. We were talking about Minju's blind date last night. I was drinking iced latte.
...

____

____

문화 Q&A

Tip or not to tip? 팁은 꼭 줘야 하는 건가요?

미국을 여행하면서 가장 곤혹스러운 것 중에 하나가 바로 팁 주기(tipping)가 아닐까 합니다. Tip은 우스갯소리로 To Insure Promptness(신속한 서비스를 위하여)의 약자라고 하는데, 팁을 많이 놓고 나가게 하기 위한 문구였다고 합니다. 요새는 한국에서도 자기가 받은 서비스에 따라 식당이나 미용실에서 약간의 팁을 놓고 나오는 사람들이 많아지고 있긴 하지만, 일반적으로 tipping이란 제도가 없는 우리나라 기준에 비추어보면 계산서 액수의 15~20%를 팁으로 얹어주는 것이 아깝게 느껴질 수 있습니다. 하지만 미국에서 tipping을 안 하면 멸시당하기 십상입니다. 그렇다면 여러 상황에서 팁의 기준은 어떻게 될까요?

우선 팁을 주는 상대는 수입을 거의 팁에 의존하는 서비스직 종사자들인데, 대표적인 예가 식당 종업원(food server), 주차요원(valet service), 짐꾼(porter), 택시운전사(taxi driver), 미용사(hair-stylist) 등입니다. 팁의 액수는 계산서가 나오는 경우(예를 들면, 식당이나 술집, 택시 등)에는 액수의 15~20%가 기준입니다. 계산서나 요금이 나오지 않는 경우(예를 들면, 호텔의 포터, 룸메이드, 주차요원 등)에는 1달러가 기준입니다.

팁을 줄 때 쓸 수 있는 유용한 표현들을 살펴볼까요?

- Keep the change, please. 거스름돈은 가지세요.

택시요금이 18달러인데, 20달러짜리 지폐를 낼 경우 쓰면 유용한 표현이겠죠?

- Is service included? 서비스(팁)가 포함된 가격입니까?

호텔이나 유명 레스토랑의 경우 팁이 계산서에 포함된 경우가 있습니다. 이럴 때는 팁을 따로 낼 필요가 없겠죠. 팁을 줘야 하는지 안 줘도 되는지 잘 모르겠으면 물어보세요.

UNIT 6

What are you going to do?

이번 주말에 무엇을 할 계획인지 생각해 보세요.

sleep all day	watch a movie	go on a date	go on a picnic
visit family	study in the library	go to a concert	help mom
attend a wedding	invite friends	cook for dinner	go shopping
stay at home and relax	clean my room		

파트너와 함께 주말의 계획에 대해 얘기해 보세요.

【Example】

A : What are you going to do this weekend?

B : I'm going to sleep all day at home. What about you?

A : I'm going to visit my grandma.

...

Conversation 1

Track 11 *What are you going to do?*

Jisu	Finally, it's Friday!
Steve	What are you going to do this weekend?
Jisu	I'm going to go to the movies on Saturday evening. Do you want to come?
Steve	Sorry, I can't. I'm going to work on my apartment.
Jisu	Really? What are you going to do?
Steve	I'm going to paint the walls in the living room. Marcos is coming to help.
Jisu	Oh, okay. Maybe next time?
Steve	Sure. Thanks.

New Vocabulary

방의 명칭을 영어로 알아봅시다.

living room 거실 bathroom 욕실 bedroom 침실 kitchen 주방 dining room 식당

You Need to Know 1

【1】be going to + 동사원형

'be going to + 동사원형'은 '~할 것이다'로 미래의 일을 나타낼 때 씁니다. 이미 정한 결심, 의도, 마음가짐을 말할 때 씁니다.

be going to + 동사원형 : ~할 것이다

- I am going to visit my mom tomorrow. 내일 엄마를 보러 갈거야.
- He is going to see the movie. 그는 그 영화를 볼거야.

Check up

같은 뜻이 되도록 빈 칸에 알맞은 말을 쓰세요.

1. 그는 새 차를 살거야. ► He ______________ buy a new car.
2. 난 도서관에서 책을 빌릴거야. ► I ____________ borrow some books at the library.
3. 저 좀 더 먹을 거에요. ► I ______________ eat some more.

【2】be going to의 부정문

be동사 다음에 not을 붙여 '~하지 않을 것이다'라고 해석합니다.

be not going to + 동사원형 : ~ 하지 않을 것이다.

• I am not going to go there. 난 거기 가지 않을거야.
• They are not going to invite Tom. 그들은 Tom을 초대하지 않을거야.

같은 뜻이 되도록 빈 칸에 알맞은 말을 쓰세요.

1. 전 이 자전거를 팔지 않을 겁니다. ► I ______________ sell this bike.
2. 우리는 서울에서 살지 않을 겁니다. ► We ______________ live in Seoul.
3. 제 아들은 그 책을 읽지 않을 겁니다. ► My son ______________ read the book.

【3】 be going to 의문문

be동사 + 주어 + going to + 동사원형? : ~할 예정이니?

• Are you going to meet her? 그녀를 만날 겁니까?
• Is Ben going to call Julie? Ben이 Julie에게 전화할 겁니까?

대답은 Yes, 주어 + be동사. / No, 주어 + be동사 + not.으로 합니다.

• Is Mary going to help John? Mary가 John을 도와 줄건가요?
  ► Yes, She is. / No, she isn't
• Are you going to fix the cabinet? 네가 장식장을 고칠거니?
  ► Yes, I am. / No, I'm not.

같은 뜻이 되도록 빈 칸에 알맞은 말을 쓰세요.

1. Smith 부인이 아이를 낳을 건가요? ► ____________ have a baby?
2. 그들은 신혼여행을 갈 건가요? ► ____________ go on a honeymoon?
3. Jane은 곧 학교를 마치나요? ► ____________ finish school soon?

【4】 Wh- be going to 의문문

What + be동사 + 주어 + going to + 동사원형? : 무엇을 할 예정입니까?

- What are you going to draw? 무엇을 그릴 겁니까?
- Who are you going to meet? 누굴 만날 겁니까?
- Where are they going to go on a honeymoon? 그들은 어디로 신혼여행을 갈 예정입니까?
- When are you going to clean your room? 넌 언제 네 방을 청소할거니?
- How long are you going to stay 얼마나 오래 머물거니?

같은 뜻이 되도록 빈 칸에 알맞은 말을 쓰세요.

1. 이번 방학 때 어디 갈거니? ► ____________ go for your vacation?
2. 저녁 때 뭘 요리할거니? ► ____________ cook in the evening?
3. 누구랑 함께 갈거니? ► ____________ go there?

Conversation 2

Track 12 *I'll call you.*

Marcos Jisu, what are you going to do this evening?

Jisu I'll probably go out tonight.

Julia invited me for dinner.

What about you, Marcos?

Marcos Oh, actually, I wanted to study together for our English test.

Jisu Right. I have to study for the test, too.

Do you think the test will be difficult?

Marcos Well, I don't think the test will be difficult.

But I have to review some grammar points.

Jisu Will you be home tonight?

Marcos Yes, I'll stay at home.

Jisu Ok. I'll call you after dinner.

New Vocabulary

probably 아마도 invite 초대하다 actually 실은 grammar 문법

You Need to Know 2

【1】 미래시제 will

'will + 동사원형'은 '~할 것이다'로 미래에 할 일을 단순히 예상할 때 씁니다. 많은 경우 'be going to + 동사원형'과 의미 차이가 거의 없지만, 미묘한 차이가 있으니 알아두도록 합니다.

- I will(= am going to) change my job. 난 직장을 바꿀(옮길)거야.
- Jason will(is going to) stay here tonight. Jason은 오늘 여기 머물거야.

'will'이 단순한 조건적인 상황에서 쓰이는데 비해 be going to는 현재에 원인이나 예측할 수 있게 하는 상황이 이미 존재하는 경우에 씁니다.

- My mom will like the TV show. 엄마는 그 TV쇼를 좋아할 거에요.
- I'm going to learn English. 전 영어를 배울 거에요.

✔ 주어 + will을 축약형으로 쓸 수 있습니다.

ex) He will love me. ► He'll love me. 그는 날 사랑할거야.

I will carry it for you. ► I'll carry it for you. 제가 들어드릴께요.

【2】 주어의 의지를 나타내는 will

'will'이 주어의 의지를 나타내며 '~하겠다', '~할 작정이다'의 의미를 나타내는 경우

- I will never forget her. 난 그녀를 결코 잊지 않을거야.
- I'll do my best. 최선을 다 할 것입니다.

【3】 추측을 나타내는 will

'will'이 추측을 나타낼 때 사용되는 경우 '아마 ~일 것이다'로 해석합니다.

- It will rain tomorrow. (아마)내일 비가 올거야.
- He will be free tonight. (아마도)그는 오늘 한가할거야.

【4】 습관이나 경향을 나타내는 will

'will'이 주어의 반복되는 습관이나 경향, 성향 등을 나타낼 때 사용될 수도 있으며, '곧잘 ~한다', '~하는 법이다'로 해석합니다.

- Accidents will happen. 사고는 일어나는 법이다.
- She will write for hours once she started. 그녀는 시작했다 하면 수시간 동안 글을 쓴다.

같은 뜻이 되도록 빈 칸에 알맞은 말을 쓰세요.

1. 그는 그 선물을 좋아할거야. ► He ________________ the present.
2. 전 아마 도서관에 갈거에요. ► I probably ________________ to the library.
3. 내가 도와줄게. ► I ________________ you.
4. 기름은 물에 뜬다. ► Oil ________________ on water.
5. 언젠가는 결혼할거야. ► Someday I ________________ married.

【5】 be going to 미래시제와 will 미래시제의 차이점

be going to + 동사원형 / will + 동사원형 모두 '~ 할 것이다'라는 의미의 미래시제를 표현하지만, 미묘한 뜻의 차이가 있습니다.

be going to + 동사원형 : 이미 결정하고 예정되어 있는 미래
will + 동사원형 : 바로 그때 결정한 의지

만약, 이번 주말에 수영장에 가기로 계획하고 있다면,

- I am going to go swimming this weekend.
  라고 얘기하지만, 날씨가 너무 더워 즉흥적으로 수영장에 갈 생각이 들었다면,
- I will go swimming this weekend.
  라고 얘기합니다.

어떠한 상황을 보고, 그 일이 막 일어날 것 같을 때도 be going to를 씁니다.

- Look at the sky. It's going to rain.
  하늘을 보니 비가 올 것 같은거죠.
- Be careful! The shelf is going to fall.
  흔들거리는 선반을 보니 선반이 떨어질 상황인 것처럼요.

I am going to see my friends.는 계획하고 친구들을 만나는 것이고 또한 계획 변동이 거의 없을 것이라는 의미를 나타냅니다. 반면에 I will see my friends.는 즉흥적으로 결정해서 친구들을 만날 것이며, 계획 변경이 가능할 수도 있다는 의미를 포함합니다.
하지만, 미래에 대한 단순한 추측일 경우에는 둘 다 비슷하게 쓰입니다.

다음의 빈 칸에 문맥에 따라 be going to 또는 will을 쓰세요.

1. I ____________________ visit my grandma for the holiday.
2. I'm really tired. I ____________________ go home and rest.
3. (Phone rings.) I ____________________ get it.

Future Plans

가능한 많은 친구들에게 방학의 계획을 물어보고 표를 완성해 봅니다. 가능한 많은 정보를 모아 보세요.

Are you going to …?	Name	Notes
travel overseas		
visit family		
meet high school friends		
study English		
get a part-time job		
read books		
learn something new		
go on a blind date		
workout		
get a certificate		
do volunteer work		
______________________		

누구의 계획이 가장 흥미로운가요? 친구들에게 소개해 주세요.

【Example】
Hanna is going to study for her MOS certificate.
She's going to study with James and they are going to …

What are you going to do on your birthday?

친구들에게 생일 때 무엇을 할 계획인지 물어 보세요.

【Example】

A : When's your birthday, George?

B : It's May 2nd.

A : What are you going to do on your birthday?

B : I'm going to invite some friends and cook dinner.

A : That's wonderful.

친구들의 계획을 적어 보세요.

Name	Name	Name

Exercises

A. 아래의 단어와 be going to를 이용하여 문장을 완성해 보세요.

watch	wear	bring	wash	help

1. What ______________________ to the party tonight?
2. I ______________________ some wine for Jack's housewarming party.
3. This new movie looks interesting. I ______________________ it.
4. My car is dirty. I ______________________ it this afternoon.
5. Linda is moving out today. I ______________________ her.

late	walk	buy	invite	do

6. ______________________ Tom to your party?
7. Oh, no! It's 9 o'clock already. I ______________________ for class.
8. I think they ______________________ home.
9. What __________ Mary ______________________ when she graduates?
10. My brother is saving money. He ______________________ new sneakers.

B. 빈 칸에 will('ll) 또는 will not(won't)를 쓰세요.

1. It's my grandma's birthday next Sunday. She __________ be 84.
2. I'm sorry. It __________ happen again.

3. Wake up early and do some exercise. You __________ feel better.

4. I'm leaving tonight for San Diego. I __________ be at home tomorrow.

5. My boss is on holiday. He __________ be back next week.

C. 빈 칸에 be going to와 괄호 안의 동사를 이용하여 대화를 완성해 보세요.

Justin What __________ you ________________ this weekend?(do)

Sarah I ____________________________ the Cats on Saturday.(see)

Justin That sounds good.

Sarah Yeah. I got a free ticket from my sister. How about you?

Justin Well, I _________________ a baseball game on TV in the afternoon.(watch)

Sarah And what __________ you ________________ in the evening?(do)

Justin I don't have anything to do.

Sarah Well, I ____________________ some friends over for a barbecue.(invite)
Do you want to come?

Justin Great. Thank you.

D. 문맥을 참고하여 빈 칸에 be going to나 will을 쓰세요.

1. A : Do you want me to help you?
B : No, thanks. Tom ________________ help me.

2. A : Would you like tea or coffee?
B : I ________________ have tea, thank you.

3. A : Do you have plans for holiday?
B : I ________________ visit my family for a few days.

4. A : Can I have a glass of water?
B : Sure. I ________________ get it for you.

5. A : We need some ink for the printer.
B : Okay. I ________________ go to the stationary.

E. 졸업 후에 무엇을 할 것인지 be going to를 이용한 문장으로 써 보세요.

1 ____

2 ____

3. ____

미국의 휴일

한국에서는 추석이 가장 큰 축제일(명절)이지만, 미국에서는 크리스마스가 가장 큰 축제일입니다. 미국에서는 축제일을 보통 월요일로 돌려서 3일간 연휴를 가집니다. 국경일은 보통 쉬게 되어 있으나, Sandwich day(샌드위치 데이 : 휴일이 화요일이나 목요일처럼 근무일 사이에 끼어 있는 경우)일 경우에도 쉬는 경우가 많습니다.

국경일이 있는 날은 보통 쉬게 되어 있으나, Floating holiday(플로팅 홀리데이 : 주중의 휴일을 주말이나 주초로 돌려 쉬는 경우)로 쉬기도 합니다. 단, 크리스마스와 독립기념일만은 이동하지 않습니다. 또한 추수감사절과 크리스마스 연휴에는 약 1주일 정도 별도의 휴가를 즐기기도 합니다. 또한 연방제 국가인 미국에서는 주나 시에 따라 축제일이 더 휴일이 더 늘어나기도 합니다.

미국의 국경일

미국의 공휴일은 지정된 날에 쉬는 것 외에 '몇째 주 월요일'과 같이 정해서 금요일부터 월요일까지 연휴로 쉴 수 있게 한 날이 많습니다. 그리고 주(州)마다 서로 다른 공휴일을 적용하기도 하지요. 다음은 미국 각 주에서 공통적으로 지키는 대표적인 공휴일입니다.

- New Year's Day(새해 첫날) : 1월 1일
- Martin Luther King Jr. Day(마틴루터킹 데이) : 1월 셋째 주 월요일

- President's Day(대통령의 날) : 2월 셋째 주 월요일
- Memorial Day(현충일) : 5월 마지막 주 월요일
- Independence Day(독립기념일) : 7월 4일
- Labor Day(노동절) : 9월 첫번 째 월요일
- Columbus Day(콜럼버스 데이) : 10월 두번 째 월요일
- Veterans Day(재향군인의 날) : 11월 11일
- Thanks Giving Day(추수감사절) : 11월 넷째 주 목요일
- Christmas Day(크리스마스) : 12월 25일

이외에도 국경일은 아니지만, 대부분의 미국인들이 지키는 기념일, 축제일도 있습니다.

- St. Valentine's Day(성 발렌타인 데이) : 2월 14일
- St. Patrick's Day(성 패트릭 데이) : 3월 17일
- Easter Sunday(부활절) : 3월 하순 ~ 4월 상순
- April Fools' Day(만우절) : 4월 1일
- Mother's Day(어머니의 날) : 5월 둘째 주 일요일
- Decoration Day(전몰장병 기념일) : 5월 마지막 주 월요일
- Flag Day(국기의 날) : 6월 14일
- Father's Day(아버지의 날) : 6월 셋째 일요일
- Halloween(할로윈) : 10월 31일

UNIT 7

Do you like sports?

계절별로 좋아하는 운동이나 운동경기에 대해 생각해 보세요.

Spring	Summer
play golf play baseball play soccer __________ __________	play volleyball play basketball go swimming __________ __________
Fall	**Winter**
go hiking go bike riding play badminton __________ __________	play ice-hockey go ice-skating go skiing __________ __________

파트너와 함께 좋아하는 운동이나 운동경기에 대해 얘기해 보세요.

【Example】

A : What sports do you like? B : I like baseball.

A : Do you? Which team do you like? B : I like LG Twins.

Conversation 1

Track 13 *I love sports.*

Jisu	So, Steve, what do you do in your free time?
Steve	Well, I love sports.
Jisu	Really? What sports do you like?
Steve	I like to play baseball.
Jisu	When do you play?
Steve	Every weekend.
Jisu	Wow, you're a really good athlete! Who do you play with?
Steve	I'm a baseball club member. I play at the Gate Park. What about you? Do you like baseball?
Jisu	No, I don't like it very much But I like to watch it on TV.

New Vocabulary

free time(= spare time) 여가시간 **athlete** 운동선수

You Need to Know 1

【1】 to부정사(infinitive; 不定詞)란?

부정사(不定詞)란 품사가 정해지지 않았다는 의미이며, to를 앞세운 부정사를 to부정사라고 합니다. 동사에 to를 붙여 만든 to부정사는 명사 자리에 놓이면 명사로 쓰이고, 형용사 자리에 놓이면 형용사로, 부사자리에 놓이면 부사로 쓰입니다.

【2】 to부정사의 명사적 용법

to부정사가 문장에서 주어, 목적어, 보어로 쓰이는 경우

- To learn other languages is difficult. 다른 언어들을 배우는 것은 어렵다.(주어)
- He refused to leave. 그는 떠나는 것을 거절했다.(목적어)
- My goal is to get a job. 나의 목표는 직업을 구하는 것이다.(보어)

✔ to부정사가 주어로 쓰이는 경우에는 그 자리에 가주어 it을 쓰고 to부정사는 문장의 뒤로 보내는 것이 일반적입니다.

ex) To say sorry is not easy

► It is not easy to say sorry. 미안하다고 말하는 것은 어렵다.

To finish the project early is his plan.

► It is his plan to finish the project early. 프로젝트를 일찍 끝내는 것이 그의 계획이다.

to부정사를 목적어로 취하는 동사

want	plan	decide	try	hope	expect	offer	need	promise
refuse	learn	choose	pretend	wish	care	ask		

다음을 우리말로 옮겨 보세요.

1. His dream was to become president. ► ______________________

2. It's not safe to travel alone. ► ______________________

3. He wants to make a lot of friends. ► ______________________

【3】 to부정사의 형용사적 용법

① to부정사가 형용사의 역할을 하는 경우
② be + to부정사로 예정, 의무, 가능, 운명, 의도 등의 의미를 나타낼 때

- I have a lot of work to do. 난 할 일이 많다.
- The refugees need something to eat. 그 난민들은 먹을 것이 필요하다.
- She is to leave for New York next week. 그녀는 다음 주에 뉴욕으로 떠날 예정이다.
- He was to be a painter. 그는 화가가 될 운명이었다.

다음을 우리말로 옮겨 보세요.

1. This is a difficult question to answer. ► ______________________

2. I have something to ask you. ► ______________________

3. I need a roommate to live with. ► ______________________

4. You are to come to the party. ► ______________________

【4】 to부정사의 부사적 용법

① to부정사가 문장에서 부사의 역할(동사, 형용사, 부사를 수식)을 하는 경우
② '~하기 위해'라는 목적, '~해서', '~하니'라는 원인을 나타내는 경우
③ '결국 ~하다(되다)'의 결과나 '~하다니'의 판단의 근거를 나타내는 경우

- I go to school to study. 나는 공부하려고 학교에 간다.
- I saved some money to buy a new car. 새 차를 사려고 돈을 모았다.
- I'm so happy to be here. 여기에 있게 되어 기쁩니다.
- James grew up to be an actor. James는 자라서 배우가 되었다.
- You must like her to say so. 그리 말하는걸 보니 그녀를 좋아하는구나.

다음을 우리말로 옮겨 보세요.

1. I'm so sorry to hear the news. ► ____________________
2. Emily came to Korea to see her friends. ► ____________________
3. He must be sick to go home early. ► ____________________
4. John must be angry to say so. ► ____________________

【5】 to부정사의 부정문

to 앞에 not(never)를 쓴다.

- She decided not to go to college. 그녀는 대학에 가지 않기로 결정했다.
- He tried not to meet her. 그는 그녀를 만나지 않으려 했다.

Conversation 2

Track 14 *I'll be busy studying.*

Steve	Do you want to get together this weekend? Marcos is coming to my house.
Jisu	Sure, but I'll be busy studying on Sunday. How about Friday night or Saturday?
Steve	Then, let's meet on Saturday. What time do you want to come?
Jisu	Well, I have to work until 5:00 on Saturday. Shall we meet at 5:30?
Steve	OK. We can watch football and play video games.
Jisu	All right. Afterward, maybe we can get some dinner.
Steve	Sounds great!

New Vocabulary

get together 모이다, 만나다 | be busy ~ing ~하느라 바쁘다
Shall we ~? 우리 ~할까? | afterward 그 후에

You Need to Know 2

【1】 동명사(Gerund : 動名詞)

동명사란 명사의 기능(주어, 목적어, 보어)을 하는 동사 형태를 말합니다. 동명사의 형태는 동사원형 + -ing이며, 앞에 not을 써서 부정의 뜻을 나타냅니다.

【2】 동명사의 역할

① '~하는 것은'의 주어 역할 ② '~하는 것을'의 목적어 역할 ③ '~하는 것이다'의 보어 역할

- Singing is my favorite hobby. 노래 부르는 것은 내가 가장 좋아하는 취미이다.
- I enjoyed watching his new movie. 나는 그의 새로운 영화를 보는 것을 즐겼다.
- My dream is being a pilot. 내 꿈은 조종사가 되는 것이다.

다음에서 맞는 동사를 골라 알맞은 형태로 써 보세요.

travel	make	wait	help

1. ___________ in a long line is boring.
2. My grandmother's dream was ___________ all around the world.
3. His goal was ___________ a lot of money.
4. Bill was interested in ___________ poor people.

【3】 자주 쓰이는 동명사 표현

be busy ~ing	~하느라 바쁘다	be worth ~ing	~할 만한 가치가 있다
How(What) about ~ing?	~하는 것은 어때?	feel like ~ing	~하고 싶다
go ~ing	~하러 가다	on ~ing	~하자마자
It is no use ~ing	~해도 소용없다	cannot help ~ing	~하지 않을 수 없다
have difficulty ~ing	~하는데 어려움을 겪다	end up ~ing	(결국)~로 끝나다
spend time(money) ~ing	~하는데 시간(돈)을 쓰다	There is no ~ing	~할 수 없다, ~하면 안 된다

【4】 동명사와 현재분사

동명사와 현재분사는 모두 '동사원형 + -ing'의 형태를 취하지만, 동명사는 명사의 역할을, 현재분사는 형용사의 역할을 합니다.

동명사 : ~하는 것 / 현재분사 : ~하고 있는 중(인)

- My favorite activity is playing basketball. 내가 가장 좋아하는 활동은 농구다.
- I'm playing basketball. 난 농구경기 중이다.

【5】 동명사와 to부정사

동사 중에는 to부정사만을 목적어로 취하는 동사, 동명사만을 목적어로 취하는 동사, 둘 다 목적어로 취하는 동사들이 있습니다.

동명사만 쓰는 동사	둘 다 쓰는 동사	to부정사만 쓰는 동사
mind, enjoy, give up, finish, deny miss, practice, consider, keep suggest, postpone	like love hate start begin regret forget	want, hope, wish, expect, decide, plan, promise, agree, learn, choose, try, need, ask manage

- Would you mind helping me?
  저 좀 도와주시겠어요?
- I couldn't finish reading the book.
  그 책을 끝까지 읽지 못했어.
- I hope to get a good job soon.
  곧 좋은 직장을 얻기 바래.
- I decided to go to the college.
  난 대학에 가기로 결정했어.

목적어로 동명사를 쓰는 동사는 이미 끝났거나 계속되는 상황을 나타내는 경우가 많으며, 목적어로 to부정사를 쓰는 동사는 미래의 뜻을 나타내는 경우가 많습니다.

목적어로 동명사가 올 때, to부정사가 올 때 뜻이 달라지는 동사들이 있습니다.

	remember	forget	try	stop
동명사	~한 것을 기억하다	~한 것을 잊다	(한 번) ~해보다	~하는 것을 멈추다
to부정사	~할 것을 기억하다	~할 것을 잊다	~하려고 노력하다	~하기 위해 멈추다

우리말과 같은 뜻이 되도록 아래에서 단어를 골라 적절한 형태로 쓰세요.

buy lock live open

1. He remembers ____________ in Japan when he was seven.
   그는 7살 때 일본에서 살았던 것을 기억한다.
2. Don't forget ____________ the door when you go out.
   나갈 때 문 잠그는 것을 잊지 마라.
3. She stopped ____________ some groceries.
   그녀는 식료품을 사기 위해 멈췄다.
4. I tried ____________ the window, but I couldn't.
   난 창문을 열려고 노력했지만 그럴 수 없었다.

Activity

What do you like?

본인이 아주 좋아하는, 좋아하는 그리고 좋아하지 않는 것들을 찾아 표를 완성해 봅니다.

	I love …	I like …	I don't like …
sports			
foods			
pet			
pastime			

파트너의 표와 비교해 보고, wh-의문문을 이용하여 궁금한 것들을 물어 보세요.

【Example】

A : What foods do you love?

B : I love Italian.

A : What Italian food do you love?

B : I love pepperoni pizza.

What kinds of movie do you like?

친구들에게 좋아하는 음악, 영화, TV 프로그램과 가수, 배우 등에 대해 물어봅니다.

[Example]

A : Do you like movies?

B : Yes, I like comedies.

A : What kinds of music do you like?

B : I like K-pop.

A : Who's your favorite singer?

친구들에게 질문을 하여 아래의 표를 완성하고, 각 그룹이 가장 좋아하는 것을 알아봅시다.

What's your favorite kind of ~?	______	______	______
music			
movie			
sports			

Who's your favorite ~?	______	______	______
singer			
actor/actress			
athlete			

Exercises

A. 밑줄 친 부분에 괄호 안의 동사를 올바른 형태로 쓰세요..

1. I want to learn ____________. (swim)
2. My boss offered ____________ me. (help)
3. Robert promised ____________ here on time. (be)
4. I suggested him ____________ in my car. (go)
5. Please stop ____________. (talk) I can't concentrate.
6. Melissa would like ____________ you. (meet)
7. My sister is very upset and refused ____________ to me. (speak)
8. Wow! I didn't expect ____________ you here. (see)
9. He was so tired, so he couldn't keep ____________. (walk)
10. We can't finish ____________ the report. (write)

B. 다음의 대화를 완성해 보세요.

Linda Andy, what do you want ____________ (do) on vacation?

Andy I'm planning ____________ (stay) at home.

I'm really tired from work.

Linda Well, I know you're tired.

But do you mind ____________ to the beach? (go)

You can take a rest there, too.

Andy That's a good idea!

I can enjoy ____________ books. (read)

C. 보기를 이용하여 문장을 완성해 보세요.

to chit chat with friends	to buy some food
to watch the movie	to get some fresh air

1. I dropped in a café ________________________.
2. I checked the newspaper ________________________.
3. My husband went to the store ________________________.
4. I opened the window ________________________.

D. 밑줄 친 부분에 알맞은 동사를 골라 바른 형태로 써 보세요.

worry	buy	cook	ski	swim

1. My mom was busy ____________ dinner.
2. The price is not bad. It's worth ____________.
3. Would you like to go ____________?
4. It's so hot today. I feel like ____________.
5. Forget it. It's no use ____________.

E. 다음의 우리말을 참고하여 영어로 말해 보세요.

1. 여가시간에 뭘 하세요? ________________________
2. 무슨 영화를 좋아하세요? ________________________
3. 많이 좋아하지는 않아요. ________________________
4. 이번 주말에 함께 모일까? ________________________
5. 난 일요일엔 공부하느라 바쁠거야. ________________________
6. 몇 시에 올래? ________________________
7. 난 5시까진 일해야 해. ________________________
8. 5:30에 만날까요? ________________________

문화 Q&A

영미인들의 풍습

중요한 시험을 볼 때 찹쌀떡을 선물하거나 결혼식에서 아들, 딸 많이 나으라고 밤이랑 대추를 던져주는 것처럼 영미에는 어떤 풍습들이 있을까요?

The morning coffee - 미국인들이 커피를 마시는 습관은 식민지시대부터 생겼다고 합니다. 전쟁으로 인해 차(tea)를 마시기 힘들어지자 커피를 마시기 시작했다고 합니다.

A visit from the stork - 한국에서는 삼신할머니가 아이를 점찍어 준다고 믿지만, 영미에서는 황새가 아이를 물어준다고 믿는답니다. 둥지를 정성껏 만드는 황새의 습성을 보고 그럴 듯하게 생겨난 믿음이 아닌가 합니다.

Baby shower - 예비엄마의 친구들이나 여성 이웃들이 예비엄마를 위한 파티를 준비하고 아기용품을 선물해 주는 자리입니다. 요즘은 남자들도 참석해서 함께 축하하는 자리로 바뀌어가고 있습니다.

The sweet sixteen party - 십대의 딱 중간인 열여섯 살을 기념하여 파티를 벌이는데, 특히 여학생들에게는 사춘기를 시작하는 의식이라고 할 수 있습니다.

Caps and gowns at graduation - 중세 유럽에서는 학자들이 검은색 모자와 가운을 썼는데, 이 전통이 현대의 고등학교나 대학의 졸업식에까지 전해 내려오고 있습니다.

Shaking hands - 우리가 고개를 숙여 인사하는 반면, 서양사람들은 공손함의 표시로 악수를 하지요. 이는 과거에 서로 손에 무기를 지니고 있지 않다는 것을 드러내기 위해 시작된 데서 유래된 행동이라고 합니다.

Thumbs up / down - 원래는 과거 로마황제가 검투사의 목숨을 살릴지 죽일지를 결정하는 표시로 사용됐다고 합니다.

The high five - 두 사람이 손바닥을 들어올려 마주치는 하이파이브는 '멋지다', '좋다'라는 의미로 사용됩니다. 고대 로마에서 황제가 칭찬의 의미로 오른쪽 팔을 들어올린 데서 유래했다고 합니다.

"Bless you!" - 상대방이 재채기를 하면 영미인들은 "God bless you!"라고 하는데, 이는 재채기를 하는 동안 순간적으로 나쁜 기운이 들어올 수 있다고 생각했던 옛 풍습에서 유래되었다고 합니다.

UNIT 8

What's Seoul like?

Warm-up

두 곳의 사진을 보고 어울리는 단어들을 골라 보세요.

quiet	noisy	beautiful	polluted	stressful
relaxing	exciting	ugly	big	safe
dangerous	comfortable	pretty	interesting	fantastic
expensive	clear			

자신이 좋아하는 장소 두 곳을 골라 파트너에게 설명해 보세요.

【Example】

A : Busan is an exciting city. It is big and the weather is nice in summer.

B : Fiji is a beautiful island. It is quiet and relaxing. The beaches are fantastic.

Conversation 1

Track 15 *It's an exciting city.*

Steve	So you are from Seoul, Jisu?
Jisu	Yeah, I'm from Seoul, Korea.
Steve	What's Seoul like?
Jisu	It's an exciting city. It's quite big and crowded.
Steve	Wow, I want to go there someday!
Jisu	Yes, you should. There are many things to see and do.
Steve	Really? What's a good time to visit?
Jisu	I think you should go there in autumn. The weather is fantastic.
Steve	It sounds perfect to me. I should plan a trip there soon.

New Vocabulary

What's ~ like? ~는 어때? quite 아주, 상당히 fantastic 굉장한, 멋진

You Need to Know 1

【1】 대명사 it

it은 대명사(代名詞)로 한 번 언급된 명사를 다시 나타낼 때 쓰입니다.

사물	I had an apple. It was delicious. 난 사과를 먹었어. 그것은 맛있었어.
동물	I saw a dog. It was so cute. 난 개를 보았어. 그것은 너무 귀여웠어.
상황	I really appreciate it. 정말로 감사합니다.
장소	I'm from Canada. It's a beautiful country. 난 캐나다 출신이야. 그곳은 아름다운 나라야.
성을 알 수 없는 사람	Who is it? 누구세요?

밑줄에 알맞은 대명사를 쓰세요.

1. A : Whose book is this?
   B : ____________ is mine.
2. This is a nice camera. Is ____________ yours?
3. I don't like that restaurant. ____________ is not clean.

【2】 가주어 it(비인칭 주어)

it은 뜻이 없는 형식상의 주어로 시간, 요일, 날짜, 거리, 날씨 등을 나타낼 때 쓰이며, '그것'이라고 해석하지 않습니다.

시간	What time is it? It's half past ten.	몇 시니? 10시 30분이야.
날짜 / 요일	What day is it? It's Thursday.	무슨 요일이니? 목요일이야.
거리	How far is it? We can walk. It's not very far.	얼마나 머니? 걸어갈 수 있어. 멀지 않아.
날씨 / 명암	It rains a lot in summer. Turn on the light. It's dark here.	여름엔 비가 많이 와. 불 좀 켜. 여긴 어둡네.
일반적 상황	It's nice to see you.	만나서 반가워요.

다음의 우리말을 보고 영어로 써 보세요.

1. 우리 집에서 3km이다. ► ______________ from our house.
2. 오늘이 월요일이니? ► ______________ today?
3. Sydney는 지금 겨울이다. ► ______________ in Sydney now.

【3】 There is / are ~

'There is(are) ~'은 '~(들)이 있다 / 존재한다'의 의미로 쓰입니다. it 구문과 마찬가지로 가주어이며 진주어는 be동사 바로 뒤에 옵니다.

> There is (a) + 명사(주어) + 장소 = (장소)에 (명사)가 있다
> There are + 복수명사(주어) + 장소 = (장소)에 (복수명사)들이 있다

- There is a man in the dining room. 식당에 남자가 있다.
- There are many big trees in the park. 공원에 큰 나무들이 많이 있다.

【4】 There is / are 부정문과 의문문

There is(are) + not(no)~ = ~(들)이 없다
Is(Are) + there + 주어? = ~이 있습니까?

- There is not much sugar in it. 거기엔 설탕이 많이 들어있지 않다.
- There are no cars on the street. 거리에 차들이 없다.
- Is there a bank near here? 근처에 은행이 있나요?
- Are there children in the school? 학교에 아이들이 있나요?

✔ 의문문에 대한 대답은, Yes, there is(are). / No, there isn't(aren't).로 합니다.

다음의 우리말을 보고 영어로 써 보세요.

1. 10시에는 기차가 없다. ► ________________ at 10:00.
2. 그 학급에는 학생이 몇 명이 있나요? ► ________________ in the classroom?
3. 냉장고에 음식이 있나요? ► ________________ in the refrigerator?

【There 구문 시제】

- 과거 : **There was/were**
  There was a train at 11. 11시에 기차가 있었다.
- 현재완료 : **There have/has been**
  There has been a lot of rain recently. 최근에 비가 많이 내렸어요.
- 미래시제 : **There will be**
  There will be rain tomorrow. 내일 비가 올 거에요.

Conversation 2

Track 16 *Are there any computers?*

Jisu calls the library.

Clerk	Central Library. Can I help you?
Jisu	Hello. I have some questions.
Clerk	Go ahead.
Jisu	Are there any computers?
Clerk	Sure. But there aren't many. There are some on the second floor.
Jisu	Are there any materials in Korean?
Clerk	No, there aren't any.
Jisu	What about cafeteria?
Clerk	Well, there's no cafeteria here. But there are some next to the building.
Jisu	I see. Thanks a lot.

New Vocabulary

Go ahead (전화에서)말씀하세요　　material 자료　　next to ~옆에

You Need to Know 2

【1】 Some and any

some과 any는 '약간의, 몇몇의'라는 의미이지만 쓰는 곳이 다릅니다. There is(are) ~ 구문과 함께 많이 쓰이며, 뒤에 셀 수 있는 명사와 셀 수 없는 명사가 모두 올 수 있기 때문에 뒤에 나오는 명사의 형태에 주의해야 합니다.

some	any
긍정문과 권유문, 요청문에 쓰입니다. I have some apples. Would you like some apples?	부정문과 의문문에 쓰입니다. I don't' have any apples. Do you have any apples?

some과 any 뒤에 셀 수 있는 복수명사가 올 때는 반드시 명사 뒤에 '-s/-es/복수명사 형태'를 씁니다. 하지만 셀 수 없는 명사가 올 때는 복수형을 쓰면 안 됩니다.

ex) I'm going to buy some clothes. / I'm not going to buy any clothes.
There's some milk in the jug. / There isn't any milk in the jug.

빈 칸에 some이나 any를 쓰세요.

1. We need ____________ money.
2. Would you like ____________ coffee?

3. Do I need ___________ document?

4. Can I have ___________ water?

5. I didn't make ___________ mistakes.

【2】How many / How much

> How much + 셀 수 없는 명사 + is there ~?
> How many + 셀 수 있는 명사의 복수 + are there ~?

- How much traffic is there in Seoul? 서울엔 얼마나 많은 교통량이 있나요?
- How many books are there? 거기엔 책이 몇 권이나 있나요?

빈 칸에 How much나 How many를 쓰세요.

1. ________________ people are there in your family?
2. ________________ ice cream is there in the freezer?
3. ________________ crime is there?
4. ________________ brothers and sisters do you have?

【3】수나 양을 나타내는 말(양화사(量化詞) : Quantifiers)

양화사는 수량사라고도 하며, 양이나 수량을 나타내는 한정사입니다. 한정사는 뒤에 나오는 명사를 한정하는 단어(구)입니다.

셀 수 있는 명사와 함께 쓰는 양화사	셀 수 없는 명사와 함께 쓰는 양화사
There are many books.	There is much traffic.
There are a lot of(= lots of) books.	There is a lot of(= lots of) traffic.
There are some books.	There is some traffic.
Are there any books?	Is there any traffic?
There are a few books.	There is a little traffic.
There are few books.	There is little traffic.
There are no books.	There is no traffic.

다음 중 알맞은 단어를 골라 문장을 완성하세요.

1. Kate has (a few / a little) books to read.
2. There aren't (many / much) people here.
3. Do you have (some / any) work to do?

Color stairs at Soho, New York City

지도를 보고 아래의 문장을 완성해 보세요.

Coffee shop
Korean Restaurant
Department Store
Drug Store
First
Second
Gas Station
Restroom
Hill Street
Post Office
Drug Store
Avenue
Library
Bank
Book Store
Avenue
STOP
Main Street
Hospital
Park

[보기]

across from	on the between
on the corner of	behind

1. The library is ________ the ________ Street.
2. The bank is ________ the library and the book store.
3. The coffee shop is ________________ Hill and First.
4. The hospital is ________________ the park on ________ Avenue.
5. The department store is ________________________ the book store.

지도에서 아래의 장소들을 찾아보고 파트너에게 위치를 묻고 대답해 봅시다.

drug store　restroom　hotel　Korean restaurant　post office

[Example]

A : Are there any drug stores?

B : Yes, there's one on Hill Street and one on First Avenue.

A : Is there a restroom?

B : Yes, there's one next to the gas station.

A Place to Visit

자신이 좋아하거나 가보고 싶은 곳을 골라 그 도시를 설명하는 짧은 글을 완성해 보세요.

【Example】

London is an exciting city with many attractions. There are a lot of tourist destinations such as London Eye, British Museum, and Big Ben. It is great to see the bridge open to let ships through.

You should …

visitlondon.com

친구들이 쓴 글을 바꿔 읽어 보고 가장 흥미로운 곳을 찾아봅니다.

Exercises

A. "It's …"를 사용하여 그림을 묘사해 보세요.

1. 

____

2. 

____

3. 

____

4. 

____

5. 

____

6. 

____

B. "It … to …" 구문을 사용하여 문장을 완성해 보세요.(보기를 참고하세요.)

glad difficult dangerous easy fun

1. 친구를 사귀기는 쉽다. _______________ make friends.
2. 다시 뵙게되어 반갑습니다. _______________ see you again.
3. 밤에 다니는 것은 위험하다. _______________ go out at night.
4. 자전거 타는 것은 재미있다. _______________ ride a bike.
5. 불어를 배우는 것은 어렵다. _______________ learn French.

C. 'there' 구문을 사용하여 문장을 완성해 보세요.

1. ____________ any theaters in this building.
이 빌딩에는 극장이 없습니다.

2. How many people ________________ in your family?
가족이 몇 명입니까?

3. ________________ a beautiful park across the hospital.
병원 건너편에 예쁜 공원이 있습니다.

4. ________________ a subway station near here?
근처에 지하철역이 있습니까?

5. ________________ any problems?
문제 있습니까?

6. ________________ a wallet on the table.
테이블 위에 지갑이 있습니다.

7. ________________ 50 states in the USA.
미국에는 50개의 주가 있습니다.

8. ________________ a lot of car accidents in downtown.
시내에는 교통사고가 많이 일어납니다.

9. How much traffic ________________?
교통량이 얼마나 많은가요?

10. ________________ much pollution in the area.
이 지역은 공해가 심합니다.

D. many나 much, How many나 How much를 써서 문장을 완성해 보세요.

1. ________________ money do you need?

2. Did you buy ________________ food?

3. There aren't ________________ hotels in this area.

4. We don't have ________________ time. Hurry up!

5. Janet doesn't know ________________ about Tom.

6. ________________ people are coming to the party tonight?

7. ________________ cups of coffee do you drink a day?

8. Do you have ________________ friends?

E. 아래 보기에서 알맞은 단어를 골라 쓰세요.

much	a lot of	few	a few	little	a little

1. We are going to have a holiday for _________ days. 며칠 휴가를 갈 거예요.
2. They are very poor. They have _________ money. 그들은 돈이 거의 없어요.
3. I speak _________ Spanish. 저는 스페인어를 조금 합니다.
4. I am lonely. I have very _________ friends. 나는 친구가 거의 없어요.
5. Sally is a quiet person. She doesn't talk _________ 그녀는 말을 많이 하지 않아요.
6. I enjoyed my vacation. I had _________ fun.

New York! New York!

미국을 상징하는 미국 최대의 도시로서, 미국의 상업, 금융, 무역의 중심지로서 경제적 수도의 역할을 담당하고 있는 뉴욕은 이외에도 대학, 연구소, 박물관, 극장, 공연장 등 미국 문화의 중심지로서도 중요한 위치를 차지하고 있습니다. 월스트리트(Wall Street)에서는 세계의 경제가, UN본부에서는 세계의 정치가 움직입니다.

Must-see NYC - Part Ⅰ

1. NYC Skyline

뉴욕시의 스카이라인은 그 자체만으로도 관광명소가 됩니다. 뉴욕의 고층 빌딩의 대부분은 20세기 초부터 현재까지 역사상 서로 다른 시대에 지어진 다양한 건축양식을 대표하는 랜드마크입니다. 특히 아르데코 건축양식의 가장 훌륭한 예로 일컬어지는 엠파이어 스테이트 빌딩(Empire State Building) 전망대(Top of the Rock)에서 바라보는 도시의 전망은 다른 어떤 곳의 전망과도 비교할 수 없습니다.

2. Time Square / Broadway

낮보다 화려한 밤, 거대한 사이즈의 광고판 및 극장간판으로 대표되는 맨하튼의 타임스퀘어는 많은 사람들이 뉴욕의 중심이자 세계의 교차로로 생각하는 곳입니다. 타임스퀘어는 또한 브로드웨이와 동일시되며 오랜 역사를 가진 극장과 최고 인기의 쇼를 볼 수 있습니다.

3. Statue of Liberty

미국 뉴욕항으로 들어오는 허드슨강 입구의 리버티 섬(Liberty Island)에 서 있는 여신상은 1886년 미국 독립 100주년을 기념하여 프랑스에서 우호증진을 위한 선물로 준 것입니다. 여신상은 외적으로는 조각이지만 내부에 계단과 엘리베이터가 설치된 건축물의 요소를 동시에 가지고 있습니다. 작가 프레데리크-오귀스트바르톨디(Frederic-Auguste Bartholdi)가 자신의 어머니를 모델로 조각했다고 하며, 에펠탑의 설계자이기도 한 귀스타브 에펠(Gustave Eiffel)이 내부 철골구조물에 대한 설계를 맡았습니다. 여신상의 왕관 부분에는 뉴욕을 내려다보는 전망대가 설치되어 있고 박물관과 선물가게도 있습니다. 1984년 유네스코 지정 세계유산에 등록되었습니다.

4. Central Park

맨하튼 중심부에 약 3.24 평방킬로미터의 넓은 면적에 펼쳐진 센트럴 파크는 오늘날 뉴욕시의 대표적인 공공 공원입니다. 센트럴파크 안에 들어서면 바쁘고 소란스러운 맨하튼 거리와 다른 곳에 있는 것처럼 여유롭고 조용합니다. 뉴요커들은 이 공원을 '도심 속의 오아시스'라고 부릅니다. 여름에는 메트로폴리탄 오페라와 뉴욕 필하모닉 오케

스트라의 무료공연이 종종 열립니다. 연못, 호수, 산책로, 잔디밭, 분수, 회전목마, 동물원, 벨베데레 성 등 공원 곳곳에 숨어 휴식처가 숨어있는 센트럴파크는 그 아름다운 풍경 때문에 여러 영화나 광고의 배경으로도 많이 등장합니다.

5. Brooklyn Bridge

브루클린 브릿지는 브루클린과 맨하튼을 연결하는 다리로 이스트 강(East River)을 가로지르며 길이가 1,828미터에 이릅니다. 다리 위에는 차도와 함께 중앙 인도에 보행자와 자전거 전용도로가 있어 방문객은 천천히 산책을 하거나 다리와 강, 뉴욕의 스카이라인을 감상할 수 있습니다.

목적지까지의 거리나 걸리는 시간을 물어볼 때 유용한 표현들을 살펴 봅시다.

A : How far is it from here to Time Square?	여기서 타임스퀘어까지 얼마나 멉니까?
B : It's quite far from here.	여기서 꽤 멀어요.
You should take a bus or a subway.	버스나 지하철을 타셔야 해요.
A : How long does it take?	얼마나 오래 걸립니까?
B : It takes about 20 minutes by bus.	버스로 20분 거리에 있어요.

참고 : 뉴욕시 공식 홈페이지 nycgo.com

UNIT

9

When was it built?

Warm-up

아래 그림을 보고 그것에 대한 설명을 골라보세요.

1. It was built with marble.
2. It was officially opened by Queen Elizabeth II in 1973.
3. They were built with brick and stone.
4. They were placed western of the river Nile.
5. It was built on a mountain.
6. It is located in India.
7. It was discovered by an American.
8. Many performances are played there.

Conversation 1

Track 17 *It was built about 2,000 years ago.*

Steve My parents are going to China next week.

Jisu Wow! That's wonderful. For holiday?

Steve Yeah. This year is their 25th wedding anniversary. And they want to visit the Great Wall.

Jisu It was built about 2,000 years ago. And it's the largest and the longest man-made wall.

Steve Right. I don't know how they built such a great structure.

Jisu Are you going to prepare anything for your parents?

Steve Well, my sister and I are planning to prepare dinner for them.

New Vocabulary

anniversary 기념일	man-made 인공의, 사람이 만든
structure 건물, 건축물	prepare 준비하다

You Need to Know 1

【1】 능동태(Active Voice)와 수동태(Passive Voice)

능동태란, 주어가 스스로 동작을 하는 문장, '주어가 ~하다'란 의미로 행동, 행위의 주체인 주어가 강조된 문장의 형태입니다.

- Henry stole the car. Henry가 차를 훔쳤다.
- Kim found the dog at the garage. Kim이 차고에서 개를 찾았다.

수동태는 문장의 주어가 동작의 영향을 받거나 당할 때, 즉 주어가 '~되다'라는 의미로 쓰이는 문장입니다. 「be동사 + 과거분사」의 형태로 쓰며 동작의 주체는 「by + 행위자」로 씁니다. 행위자가 일반적인 사람들, 불명확한 경우, 누구나 알 수 있는 사람 등이라면 생략할 수 있습니다.

- A lot of teenagers read this book.
  - ► This book is read by a lot of teenagers. 이 책은 많은 10대들에 의해 읽혀진다.
- Carl takes care of the baby.
  - ► The baby is taken care of by Carl. 이 아기는 carl에 의해 보살핌을 받는다.

✔ 과거분사 만드는 법

<규칙동사> 대부분의 동사는 동사의 기본형에 -ed를 붙입니다. 동사의 과거형과 형태가 같습니다.	<불규칙동사> 몇몇 동사들은 원형동사 또는 과거형 동사와 전혀 다른 형태로 변합니다.
call → called	be → been
like → liked	go → gone
hop → hopped	eat → eaten
study → studied	make → made

다음을 수동태로 바꾸어 보세요.

1. I clean my room everyday. ► ____________________
2. Many people use smart phones. ► ____________________
3. Ed kisses her. ► ____________________

【2】 과거, 진행, 미래 시제의 수동태

- I was born in Seoul. 전 서울에서 태어났어요.
- My car is being repaired. 제 차는 수리되고 있어요.
- Tony was being examined by the doctor. Tony는 의사로부터 검진을 받고 있었어요.
- The report will be finished by the manager. 그 리포트는 매니저에 의해 마무리될 것이다.

다음을 수동태로 바꾸어 보세요.

1. Shakespeare wrote King Lear. ► ____________________
2. Someone took this seat. ► ____________________
3. She is cooking dinner. ► ____________________
4. The police caught the thief. ► ____________________
5. Everybody will remember you. ► ____________________

【3】 수동태의 부정문과 의문문

- Monica was not awarded a medal.　Monica는 메달을 받지 못했다.
- Was he beaten by the robber?　그가 강도에게 맞았나요?

다음을 부정문으로 바꾸어 보세요.

1. The dog is punished again. ► ______________________
2. This seat is taken. ► ______________________
3. They were arrested for a crime. ► ______________________

다음을 의문문으로 바꾸어 보세요.

1. Many cars are exported nowadays. ► ______________________?
2. They were surrounded by the enemy. ► ______________________?
3. My sister was fired from her job. ► ______________________?

Conversation 2

Track 18 *Which is bigger?*

Steve Let's try this quiz on the paper.
Are you ready?

Jisu Okay. Go ahead.

Steve First question. Which planet is bigger, the earth or Mars?

Jisu Hmm, I think the earth is bigger.

Steve Right. Mars is not as big as the earth.
I have another question.
What's the longest river in the U.S.?

Jisu Is it the Mississippi river?

Steve That's right! It's 3,730km long.
Which is the smallest country in the world?

Jisu I'm not sure. Is it Monaco?

Steve Ah··· no. It's Vatican City.

New Vocabulary

Go ahead 어서 하세요. Mars 화성

You Need to Know 2

【1】 비교급과 최상급

- He is taller than me.
  그는 나보다 키가 더 크다.
- This red car is more expensive than the black one.
  이 빨간 차가 검정색 차보다 더 비싸다.
- Russia is the largest country in the world.
  러시아는 세계에서 가장 큰 나라이다.

비교급, 최상급을 만드는 규칙

	원급	비교급	최상급
대부분의 형용사(부사) : 원급 +er, est	cold fast	colder faster	coldest fastest
'단모음 + 단자음'으로 끝나는 1음절의 형용사(부사) : 자음 한 번 더 쓰고 +er, est	big hot	bigger hotter	biggest hottest
y로 끝나는 형용사(부사) : y를 i로 고치고 +er, est	pretty heavy	prettier heavier	prettiest heaviest
-ous, -ful, -ish, -less, -ly 등으로 끝나는 2음절어 또는 3음절 이상의 형용사(부사) : more + 원급 / most + 원급	beautiful stylish lovely expensive	more beautiful more stylish more lovely more expensive	most beautiful most stylish most lovely most expensive
불규칙 변화	good bad many(much) little far	better worse more less farther(거리) further(정도)	best worst most least farthest furthest

다음 빈 칸에 알맞은 단어를 쓰세요.

1. Summer is ________ ________ season. 여름은 가장 더운 계절이다.

2. Seoul is ________ ________ Hong Kong. 서울은 홍콩보다 더 크다.

3. Janet is ________ ________ girl in school. Janet은 학교에서 가장 빠른 소녀이다.

【2】 원급 비교

원급 비교란 형용사나 부사의 어형을 변화시키지 않고 'as ~ as' 구문을 이용하여 비교하는 것입니다.

- Cathy is as pretty as Cindy. Cathy는 Cindy만큼 예쁘다.
- She is not as(so) pretty as Betty. 그녀는 Betty만큼 예쁘지 않다.

다음 빈 칸에 알맞은 단어를 쓰세요.

1. I study _____ _____ _____ my sister. 나는 우리 언니만큼 열심히 공부한다.

2. He is _____ _____ _____ Mike. 그는 Mike만큼 키가 크다.

3. Ben is _____ _____ _____ his brother. Ben은 그의 형만큼 똑똑하다.

【3】 관용어구

as soon as possible	가능한 한 빨리	as proud as a peacock	공작처럼 뽐내는
as busy as a bee	벌처럼 바쁜	as sly as a fox	여우처럼 교활한
as easy as pie	식은 죽 먹기		

- These questions are as easy as pie. 이 문제들은 식은 죽 먹기에요.
- Come home as soon as possible. 가능한 집에 빨리 와라.

Activity

Which is better?

아래의 표를 비교해 보고 각 그룹에서 수학여행을 갈만한 가장 좋은 플랜을 골라봅니다.

Plan A

Destination	Price	Transportation	Accommodation	Includes
Busan	₩150,000	Train	3 star hotel	Train tickets 2 days accommodation Breakfast City tour

Plan B

Destination	Price	Transportation	Accommodation	Includes
Jeju	₩350,000	Plane	3 star hotel	Air tickets 3 days accommodation Breakfast City tour

Plan C

Destination	Price	Transportation	Accommodation	Includes
Jeju	₩500,000	Plane	4 star hotel	Air tickets 3 days accommodation Breakfast / dinner City tour Museum ticket Airport ride

그룹에서 결정한 플랜이 왜 좋은지 발표해 봅시다.

Famous Buildings

우리나라의 건축물 중 외국 친구에게 소개하고 싶은 건축물을 골라 아는대로 써 보세요.

[Example]
Changdeokgoong is a secondary palace of Choseon Dynasty. It was built by King Taejong about 600 years ago. It is located in Seoul near Gyeongbokgung. It has a beautiful back garden and it was listed in as a World Cultural Heritage by UNESCO.

____

____

____

Exercises

A. 다음의 문장을 수동태 문장으로 바꾸어 써 보세요.

1. Many Americans love Korean food nowadays.
   ► ____
2. We call him a walking dictionary.
   ► ____
3. Thousands of people visit this museum every year.
   ► ____
4. Ms. Kim designed this dress.
   ► ____
5. My dad built this house 10 years ago.
   ► ____

B. 괄호 안의 단어를 이용하여 대화를 완성해 보세요.

Grace　How was your vacation Emily??

Emily　Oh, I had a terrible vacation!

Grace　Oh, really? What happened?

Emily　Our flight ________ ________ due to bad weather. (cancel)
So we had to stay overnight at the airport.

Grace　That's terrible!

Emily　Yes. And that's not all.
My dad ________ ________ from car accident. (injure)

Grace　That's too bad. Is he alright now?

Emily　No, he's still in the hospital.
He ________ ________ ________ in a week. (discharge)

C. 한국에 관해 아래 질문에 대한 대답을 써 보세요.

1. What is the largest city?
   ► ____________________
2. How big is the largest city?
   ► ____________________
3. What is the hottest month?
   ► ____________________
4. What is the coldest month?
   ► ____________________
5. What is the most beautiful city to visit?
   ► ____________________

D. 다음의 빈칸에 as나 than을 넣으세요.

1. My bag is little heavier ________ yours.
2. Brian is smarter ________ James.
3. I didn't get up ________ early as you.
4. I feel better ________ I felt yesterday.
5. Brazil isn't as big ________ Canada.

E. 아래 보기에서 알맞은 단어를 골라 쓰세요.

best	further	farther	less	better

1. This is much ________ than that. 이게 저것보다 훨씬 낫다.
2. I can't go any ________. 더는 못가겠어
3. Contact me for ________ details. 더 자세한 사항은 저한테 연락하세요.

4. We have ________ than thirty minutes. 우린 30분도 안남았다.

5. Mr. Thomson sells only the ________ quality products.

Thomson씨는 최상의 제품만을 판매한다.

F. 다음의 우리말을 참고하여 영어로 말해 보세요.

1. 우리 부모님이 다음주에 중국에 가셔.

► ______________________________

2. 올해가 우리 부모님 25주년 결혼기념일이야.

► ______________________________

3. 그 빌딩은 100년 전에 지어졌어.

► ______________________________

4. 화성은 지구만큼 크지 않다.

► ______________________________

5. 미국에서 가장 긴 강은 무엇인가요?

► ______________________________

6. 세계에서 가장 작은 나라는 어디인가요?

► ______________________________

7. 그것은 서울에 위치하고 있습니다.

► ______________________________

8. 많은 공연이 그 곳에서 펼쳐집니다.

► ______________________________

New York! New York!

Must-see NYC - Part Ⅱ

6. Wall Street

세계 금융시장의 중심지로 세계 제일의 규모를 자랑하는 증권거래소부터 세계 유수의 금융기관이 모여 있는 세계 자본주의의 총본산이라고 할 수 있습니다.

7. Museum Mile

맨해튼의 센트럴 파크와 맞닿아 있는 5th 애비뉴의 82번가와 105번가 사이에 펼쳐지는 거리는 10여 개의 박물관이 집단적으로 뉴욕시의 가장 훌륭한 예술, 역사, 디자인 및 문화의 컬렉션을 제공하면서 뮤지엄 마일을 형성했습니다.

뮤지엄 마일의 하단부에는 세계적으로 유명한 메트로폴리탄 박물관(Metropolitan Museum of Art)이 위치하고 있으며, 여기에는 덴두르의 유명한 성전을 강조한 고대 이집트의 공예품 및 미술 컬렉션을 비롯하여 2백만 점 이상의 예술작품이 보관되어 있습니다. 예술과 건축을 사랑하는 애호가라면, 미술관 건축물 자체만으로도 유명한 솔로몬 R. 구겐하임 미술관(The Solomon R. Guggenheim Museum)을 방문해 보세요.

wikipedia.org

8. Staten Island Ferry

스태튼 아일랜드 페리는 교통수단일 뿐만 아니라 그 자체가 관광명소입니다. 방문객들은 로어 맨해튼(Lower Manhattan)에서 스태튼 아일랜드까지 항해하며 자유의 여신상, 뉴욕항의 아름다운 모습 및 맨해튼의 스카이 라인까지 즐길 수 있기 때문입니다. 게다가 요금은 무료입니다.

wikipedia.org

9. Rockefeller Center

동서로는 5번가와 7번가, 남북으로는 47번가와 52번가 사이에 21개의 빌딩으로 이루어진 록펠러센터는 도시 안의 도시라고 불리울 만큼 큰 규모입니다. 40곳 이상의 식당과 100여 곳 이상의 상점이 있어 식사와 쇼핑을 즐길 수도 있습니다. 가장 높은 빌딩은 70층 높이의 GE빌딩이며, GE빌딩과 채널 가든 사이의 광장은 여름에는 야외 카페로, 겨울에는 아이스링크로 사용되며 크리스마스 시즌에는 화려하고 거대한 트리장식이 불을 밝힙니다. NBC 방송국과 라디오시티 뮤직홀(Radio City Music Hall)도 여행자들이 많이 찾는 명소입니다.

10. Sports

뉴욕시는 다양한 스포츠 종목의 프로팀을 홈으로 보유하고 있습니다. 뉴욕시의 메이저리그 야구팀인 메츠(New York Mets)와 2009년 월드 챔피언 양키스(New York Yankees)는 뉴욕의 상징이기도 합니다. NBA의 닉스(New York Knicks)와 레인저(New York Rangers) 아이스 하키팀은 메디슨 스퀘어 가든(Madison Square Garden)에서 경기를 합니다. 이외에도 미국 오픈 테니스대회, 뉴욕시 마라톤대회 등 세계적으로 명망 높은 대회와 이벤트를 많이 개최하고 있습니다.

Let's English

UNIT

10

What would you like to eat?

아래의 사진을 보고 어떤 음식인지, 무엇으로 만들어졌는지 얘기해 봅니다.

1. 

____

2. 

____

3. 

____

4. 

____

5. 

____

6. 

____

a. It is a Korean traditional side dish.
b. It is one of the most famous Japanese dish.
c. You can add any filling you like between slices of bread.
d. You have to stir well before eating.
e. It is rounded bread topped with tomato sauce and cheese.
f. It is sour and spicy.
g. It is cooked rice in vinegar and wrapped with raw fish.
h. It is oven-baked.
i. It is a popular lunch menu.
j. It is a Korean dish made from sweet potato noodles.
k. It is cooked rice with mixed vegetables.
l. It is stir fried in sesame oil with various vegetables and meat.

이 밖에 다른 좋아하는 음식에 대해 얘기해 보세요.

Conversation 1

Track 19 *Can we go out to dinner?*

Steve Can we go out to dinner tonight?

Jisu Good idea!

Steve What do you think of Thai food?

Jisu Sorry, but I'm not really in the mood for Thai today. It's a bit spicy.

Steve Then, how do you like Chinese food?

Jisu Well, I don't feel like eating greasy food, either.

Steve Hmm. Then, you should try Japanese food.

Jisu Oh, I like it a lot.

Steve Okay, let's go. I know a great place. It's my treat!

New Vocabulary

in the mood for ~ ~할 기분이 나다
either (부정문에서) ~역시 그렇다
spicy 양념맛이 강한
feel like ~ing ~하고 싶다
greasy 기름기가 많은
treat 대접하다, 한턱 내다

You Need to Know 1

【1】 조동사 can의 용법

조동사 can은 '~ 할 수 있다'라는 의지, '~ 일 수 있다'라는 가능성, '~할 수 있다, 해도 된다'의 허락의 의미를 담고 있습니다. 조동사 can 다음에는 동사의 기본형을 쓰며, 부정형은 'cannot(can't) + 동사원형', 의문형은 'Can + 주어 + 동사원형 ~?'입니다.

① 능력 : ~할 수 있다(= be able to)
- Can you drive? 너 운전할 수 있어?
- I can help you. 널 도울 수 있어.

② 가능성 : ~일 수 있다(일어날 가능성이 있을 때)
- How can it be possible? 그게 어떻게 가능하니?
- It can be very cold in winter. 겨울에는 굉장히 추워질 수 있다.

③ 허락 : ~할 수 있다, ~해도 된다
- You can take pictures here. 여기서 사진 찍어도 됩니다.
- We can't wear jeans at the office. 우리는 사무실에서 청바지를 입을 수 없어.

④ 추측 : (부정문에서) ~일리가 없다
- That can't be James. He's in New York. 그 사람이 James일리 없어. 그는 뉴욕에 있는 걸.
- It can't be true! 그게 진실일리 없어!

다음의 우리말을 참고하여 영어로 말해 보세요.

1. 내 펜을 써도 돼. ► ______________________

2. 그게 진실일까? ► ____________________

3. 그녀는 4개국어를 할 수 있어. ► ____________________

【2】 조동사 could의 용법

could는 can의 과거형 또는 '~일 수도 있다'의 추측을 나타낼 때 사용합니다.

① can의 과거형 : ~할 수 있었다.

- I could see the sun rise from my hotel. 호텔에서 일출을 볼 수 있었어요.
- I couldn't swim when I was young. 어렸을 때 저는 수영을 할 수 없었어요.

② 추측(가능성) : ~일 수도 있다.(can보다 약한 추측)

- My mom could be right. 엄마 말씀이 맞을 수 있어요.
- He could win the lottery. 어쩌면 복권에 당첨되었을 수도 있어.

③ 허가/요청 : ~해도 될까요? / ~해 주시겠어요?

- Could I have a look? 제가 좀 봐도 될까요?
- Could you open the window? 창문 좀 열어주시겠어요?

✔ 공손의 의미로 사용되는 could는 can보다 더 공손한 느낌이 납니다. 이때는 can의 과거시제가 아닙니다.

다음의 우리말을 참고하여 영어로 말해 보세요.

1. 제시간에(on time) 거기 도착하지 못했어. ► ____________________

2. 제게 10달러만 빌려주실(lend) 수 있으세요? ► ____________________

3. 네가 원한다면, 내가 할 수도 있어. ► ____________________, if you want.

【3】 조동사 should의 용법

should는 '~해야 한다'는 의미로 의무, 필요를 나타냅니다.

- You should say sorry to mom. 엄마에게 미안하다고 얘기해야지.
- You should try it. 시도해 봐야지.

should의 부정형은 should not(shouldn't) + 동사원형으로 '~하면 안된다'는 금지를 나타내며, 의문형은 'Should + 주어 + 동사원형~?'입니다.

- You shouldn't call him at this hour. 이 시간에 그에게 전화하면 안된다.
- What should we do now? 우리 지금 뭐해야 합니까?

✔ should는 must와 의미가 비슷하지만 must보다는 의무의 정도가 약하며, 충고나 권유를 나타낼 때 씁니다.

다음 빈칸에 should나 shouldn't 중 알맞은 말을 골라 문장을 완성하세요.

1. You ____________ study hard to pass the exam.
2. Be quiet. You ____________ make a noise in the library.
3. Paul looks tired. He ____________ go home and rest.
4. It's raining outside. You ____________ bring umbrella.
5. You ____________ touch paintings in the gallery.

Conversation 2

Track 20 *May I take your order?*

Waiter Good evening. May I take your order?

Steve Yes. I'd like katsudon, please.

Waiter All right. How about you, ma'am?

Jisu Well, I'll have tempura udon, please.

Waiter Would you like anything to drink?

Jisu Green tea, please.

Steve I'll have the same.

Waiter Any dessert? We have excellent home-made ice cream.

Jisu No, thank you.

Steve Hmm, I think I'll have one.

New Vocabulary

home-made 직접 만든

You Need to Know 2

【1】 조동사 would의 용법

조동사 would는 will의 과거형이지만, 그 외의 용법으로 영미인들이 평상시에 많이 쓰는 말입니다.

① **will의 과거형 :** 조동사 will의 과거형으로 '~였을 것이다'하고 과거의 일을 짐작할 때, 또는 '~하려 했다'는 주어의 과거 의지를 나타낼 때 사용합니다.

- I think I will pass the exam. 난 내가 시험에 통과할거라 생각해.(현재)
- I thought I would pass the exam. 난 내가 시험에 통과할거라 생각했어.(과거의 일을 짐작)
- He said he would come to Korea. 그는 한국에 올거라고 말했다.(주어의 과거 의지)

② **과거의 습관 :** '~하곤 했다'라는 의미로 과거 일을 회상할 때 쓰입니다.

- He would take a walk after dinner. 그는 저녁식사 후 산책을 하곤 했다.
- My mom would visit Paris every winter. 어머니는 겨울마다 파리에 가곤 하셨다.

③ **(부정문에서) 거절, 고집(= not willing to ~할 의향이 없다)**

- Peter would not call his boss. Peter는 상사에게 전화하지 않을거야.
- She wouldn't tell me about it. 그녀는 말하려 하지 않을거야.

✔ 조동사는 항상 형태가 일정합니다. 그래서 주어가 3인칭 단수라도 s를 붙이지 않으며 뒤에는 항상 동사 원형이 옵니다. 부정문을 만들 때는 조동사 뒤에 not을 붙여주면 됩니다.

- She will not(= won't) come. 그녀는 오지 않을거야.

Tips

would + 동사원형 외에 「used to + 동사원형」 형태 또한 과거의 습관적인 동작이나 상태를 나타냅니다.

ex) He **used to** play tennis every morning. 그는 아침에 테니스를 치곤 했다.

There **used to** be a playground here. (전에는)여기에 운동장이 있었다.

④ **would like + 명사 / would like to + 동사원형** : '~하고 싶다'의 공손한 표현

- Would you like some coffee? 커피 좀 하시겠어요?
- I'd like some coffee, please. (would = 'd) 커피 좀 마시고 싶은데요.

✔ would like to는 want to와 같은 뜻이지만 보다 정중한 표현입니다.

- Would you like to join us? 저희와 함께 하실래요?
- I'd like to buy this shirt. 이 셔츠를 사고 싶은데요.

⑤ **would rather + 동사원형** : '~을 더 좋아하다'의 공손한 표현

- I would rather stay here. 난 여기 있는게 더 낫겠다.
- Would you rather go home? 집에 가는게 더 좋아요?

⑥ **would you mind + ~ing?** : ~해 주시겠습니까?(매우 정중한 표현)

- Would you mind speaking quietly? 조용히 말씀해 주시겠습니까?
- Would you mind not smoking? 금연해 주시겠습니까?

✔ mind는 허락을 구하거나 정중히 부탁을 할 때 사용하는 동사로 동명사를 취합니다. '언짢아하다', '꺼려하다'라는 의미가 있기 때문에 긍정의 대답은 부정으로, 부정의 대답은 긍정으로 해야 합니다.

ex) Would you mind opening the window? 창문을 열어주시겠어요?(창문 열기 꺼리세요?)
No, I don't mind.(= Of course not.) 아니오. 꺼리지 않습니다.(물론 아니죠.)

우리말을 참고하여 빈칸에 알맞은 단어를 쓰세요.

1. 자는게 낫겠어.
   ► I ____________________ sleep.
2. 영화를 보고 싶어요.
   ► I ____________________ to see a movie.
3. 토요일에 무엇을 하고 싶으세요?
   ► What ______________ you ______________ to do on Saturday?

4. 난 차라리 사실을 얘기할래.

► I ________________ tell the truth.

5. 어디에 가고 싶으세요?

► Where ____________ you ____________ to go?

6. 문을 닫아 주시겠습니까?

► ____________ you mind ____________ the door?

【2】 조동사 may의 용법

may는 허가, 불확실한 추측을 나타냅니다. 의문문으로 사용되는 경우

① 허가 : ~해도 좋다

- May I go out? 저 나가도 되요?
- May I use your phone? 전화를 사용해도 될까요?

② 불확실한 추측 : ~일지도 모른다.(조동사 might도 같은 의미로 쓰입니다.)

- It may snow tomorrow. 내일 눈이 올지도 모른다.
- I may go to the movies tonight. 난 오늘밤 영화 보러 갈지도 몰라.

Check up

다음의 대화를 자연스럽게 만들어 보세요.

1. A : Who is she?

 B : I'm not sure. She ____________________ Mike's girl friend.

 잘 모르겠어. 아마도 Mike의 여자친구인 것 같은데.

2. A : Did you know that Colin got an accident?

 B : Yes, I did. But it ____________________ true.

 응, 알아. 하지만 사실이 아닐 수도 있어.

Eating habits

친구들에게 아래의 질문을 물어보고 대답해 보세요.

Question / Name	______	______	______
1. What kind of food do you like to eat out?			
2. Why do you like it?			
3. Where do you usually go?			
4. Who do you go out with?			
5. Do you know any good restaurant?			

여러분이 이탈리아 식당에 있다고 생각하고, 손님과 서버가 되어 역할극을 해 봅니다.

【Example】

A : May I take your order?

B : Yes. I'd like spaghetti.

A : All right. Would you like salad?

B : No, thanks.

A : How about dessert?

...

Exercises

A. can, can't, could, couldn't와 보기의 동사를 사용하여 문장을 완성해 보세요.

hear	go	sleep	decide	eat

1. It's noisy here. I ________________________ you. Speak up, please.
2. I was very tired, but I ________________________
3. I don't know what to do. I ________________________
4. Steve ________________________ to the concert next Friday. He has to work.
5. I was so full. I ________________________ any more.

B. would, will, I'd, 또는 I'll을 넣어 아래 대화를 완성해 보세요.

Waiter What ____________ you like to eat?
Guest ____________ have New York steak.
Waiter How ____________ you like your steak?
Guest Well done, please.
Waiter Sure. Anything to drink?
Guest Yes, please. ____________ like some water.
Waiter All right. Anything else?
Guest No, thank you. That ____________ be all.

C. should나 shouldn't를 사용하여 아래 대화를 완성해 보세요.

Owen Hi, Grace. How are you?
Grace Not so good. I have a cold.

Owen	Really? That's too bad. You ________ take a rest.
Grace	I know. But I have many things to do.
Owen	Well, you ______ drink a lot of liquids. You ________ stay dry.
Grace	Oh, Ok. Thanks for the advice.

D. should와 may(might)를 써서 영작해 보세요.

ex) I think you should work hard.

1. I think everybody should ________________
2. I think I should ________________
3. He may ________________
4. She might ________________

E. 다음의 우리말을 참고하여 영어로 말해 보세요.

1. 오늘밤 저녁 먹으러 갈래?
   ► ________________
2. 한국 음식은 어떻게 생각해?
   ► ________________
3. 미안하지만 오늘은 한국음식이 별로 당기지 않아.
   ► ________________
4. 좀 달아.
   ► ________________
5. 중국음식은 좋아하세요?
   ► ________________

문화 Q&A

미국의 교육제도

미국의 교육제도는 주에 따라 다르나 대부분의 주에서 12년제의 의무교육을 실시합니다. 의무교육은 초등학교 6~8년, 중학교 4년, 고등학교 2~4년으로 나누어지고 대부분의 학생들은 17, 18세까지 학교에 다닙니다. 고등학교 과정에는 대학진학 준비과정 · 상업과정 · 교직과정 · 일반교양과정의 4개 과정이 있으며 대학은 4년제와 2년제의 초급대학이 있습니다. 국제적으로 높은 평가를 받고 있는 종합대학으로는 아이비리그라고도 불리우는 하버드, 예일, 프린스턴, 스탠퍼드, 캘리포니아대학교 등이 있고, 공학계로는 매사추세츠 공과대학교(MIT)가 널리 알려져 있지요.

미국교육의 가장 큰 특징이라고 한다면 학생 중심의 교육(student-centered education)을 들 수 있습니다. 학생 중심의 교육이란 학생들 개인의 특수성을 인정하고 개인의 소질과 능력을 충분히 발휘할 수 있도록 학교가 도와주는 역할을 한다는 말입니다. 특히, 미국에서는 정부차원에서 교육제도나 교육과정, 교육방법에 획일적인 기준을 제시하지 않고 각 주(state)와 지역(region), 학교(school) 차원의 자율성을 강조함으로써 다양한 교육방법으로 학생들의 창의성(creativity)을 길러 내는 것을 가장 중요하게 여깁니다.

아이비리그(Ivy-league)

Brown University
In God we hope

Columbia University
In thy Light we seethe light

Dartmoth University
A voice crying
in the wilderness,
The voice f one crying in
the wilderness

Harvard University
Truth

University of Pennsylvania
Laws with out morals
are useless

Princeton
Under Gods power
she flourishes

Yale
Light and truth

Cornel University
I would found an institution
where any person can find
instruction in any study

미국동부에 있는 8개 명문 사립대학교 브라운(Brown) · 컬럼비아(Columbia) · 코넬(Cornell) · 다트머스(Dartmouth) · 하버드(Harvard) · 펜실베이니아(Pennsylvania) · 프린스턴(Princeton) · 예일(Yale)대학교를 총칭하는 아이비 리그(Ivy League)는 이들 대학교에 담쟁이덩굴(ivy)로 덮인 건물이 많은 데서 유래하였다고 합니다. 1954년 8개 대학교가 '아이비 그룹 협정(Ivy Group Agreement)'을 맺고 1년에 한 번씩 미식축구 경기를 열기로 함으로써 아이비리그가 시작되었습니다. 이후 점차 스포츠의 영역을 넘어서 조직의 구성체인 '명문' 사립대학을 가리키는 일반적 호칭이 되었습니다. "아이비리그"라는 용어는 학문적 우수성, 까다로운 입학조건, 사회 엘리트주의의 다른 의미로도 쓰입니다.

Princeton University

UNIT

11

I wish I could.

Warm-up

여러분에게 아래의 일들이 벌어진다면 무엇을 하겠습니까?

rich　　tall　　pretty

have a sports car

a movie star

If I were(was) rich, I could travel all around the world.
If I were(was) tall, I could be a basketball player.

【Example】

Q : What would you do if you were rich?

A : ______________________________

Conversation 1

Track 21 *What would you do?*

Steve	Look at this! There's a talent show.
Jisu	Oh, yes. And there are prizes, too.
Steve	Do you want to enter? What are you good at?
Jisu	Oh, no. I don't think I can do that.
	Why don't you enter, Steve?
	You're a good guitar player.
Steve	Yeah. I'll consider.
Jisu	What would you do if you won the contest?
	The winner will get $1,000.
Steve	Well, if I won the contest, I would buy a new laptop.

New Vocabulary

talent show 장기자랑 be good at ~ing ~를 잘하다, ~에 능숙하다 consider 고려하다

You Need to Know 1

【1】 가정법 과거(Subjunctive Past)

현재 사실과 반대되는 상황을 가정하거나 실현 가능성이 희박한 일을 나타낼 때 가정법 과거 형태를 사용합니다. if 가정법 과거는 과거의 의미가 있는 것이 아니라 조건절에 과거형 동사를 사용하기 때문에 '가정법 과거'라고 합니다.

If + 주어 + 과거형 동사, 주어 + would / could / might + 동사원형 : 만약 ~라면, ~할텐데

- If I were taller, I would ask her to go out.
  키가 좀더 컸더라면, 그녀와 데이트 할 수 있었을텐데.
- If Phil were here, he could help us.
  Phil이 여기 있었다면, 우리를 도울 수 있었을텐데.

✔ 가정법 과거에서 if절의 be동사는 주어의 인칭에 관계 없이 항상 were를 씁니다. 하지만 최근에는 주어의 인칭에 맞추어 was를 쓰는 경우도 많이 있습니다.

다음 우리 말과 같은 뜻이 되도록 문장을 완성하세요.

1. 네가 공부를 더 열심히 한다면 그 시험에서 A를 받을 수 있을텐데.
   If you ____________ harder, you ____________ ____________ an A on the test.
2. 내가 너라면, 나는 그 일을 하지 않을텐데.
   If I ____________ you, I ____________ ____________ it.
3. 돈이 충분히 있다면, 그 차를 살텐데.
   If I ____________ enough money, I ____________ ____________ that car.

4. 내게 남자친구가 있다면, 그를 너에게 소개시켜 줄텐데.

If I ___________ a boyfriend, I ___________ ___________ him to you.

5. 그 콘테스트에서 우승을 한다면, 무엇을 할거니?

What ___________ you ___________ if you ___________ the contest?

【2】 가정법 과거완료(Subjunctive Past Perfect)

과거 사실과 반대되는 상황을 가정할 때 가정법 과거완료 형태를 사용합니다.

If + 주어 + had + p.p., 주어 + would / could / might + have p.p. : 만약 ~했다면, ~했을텐데

- If you had told me, I would have helped you.
  네가 말했더라면, 너를 도왔을텐데.
- If they had studied, they would have passed the exam.
  그들이 공부를 했더라면, 시험에 통과할 수 있었을텐데.

다음 우리 말과 같은 뜻이 되도록 문장을 완성하세요.

1. 그녀가 전화벨 소리를 들었었다면, 전화를 받았을텐데.

If she ________ ________ the phone ring, she ________ ________ ________ it.

2. 오늘 비가 왔었다면, 그 경기는 취소되었을텐데.

If it ________ ________ today, the game ________ ________ ________ ________

3. 우리가 지하철을 탔었더라면, 좀 더 빨리 도착했었을텐데.

If we ________ ________ the subway, we ________ ________ ________ there quicker.

【3】 조건의 부사절을 이끄는 if / unless

예전에는 가정법 현재라고 하여, 말하는 내용의 반대상황을 가정하여 그것을 바라고 있을 때 사용하곤 하였으나, 현대 영어에서는 거의 다루지 않고, 조건의 부사절로 보고 있습니다.

- If you are tired, we will stop doing this.
  네가 피곤하다면, 이걸 그만둘께.
- If they help us, we will be able to finish it sooner.
  그들이 우릴 도와준다면, 더 빨리 끝낼 수 있을거야.

unless는 if ~ not과 같은 의미로 '만약 ~하지 않으면'으로 해석합니다.

- You can't travel abroad, unless you have a passport.
  여권을 갖고 있지 않으면 해외여행을 할 수 없다.
- It's difficult to do, unless you're a professional.
  그건 프로가 아니면 하기 어려워요.

다음 우리 말과 같은 뜻이 되도록 문장을 완성하세요.

1. 배가 고프면, 뭘 좀 먹으렴.
   ________ ________ ________ ________, have something to eat.
2. 질문 있으면 내게 전화해.
   ________ ________ ________ ________ ________, give me a call.
3. 서두르지 않으면, 비행기를 놓칠거야.
   You'll miss the plane, ________ ________ ________ ________

Conversation 2

Track 22 *I wish I could.*

Jisu	So, are you still living with your parents, Steve?
Steve	Yes. I wish I had my own apartment.
Jisu	Why? Don't you like living with your family?
Steve	It's OK, but my mom's always nagging at me.
Jisu	Well, you know, parents are like that.
Steve	And my dad expects me to help around the house. They still talk as if I were an 8-year-old boy.
Jisu	So are you planning to move out?
Steve	I wish I could. But the rents are high. I wish life weren't so difficult.

New Vocabulary

nag at ~에게 성가시게 잔소리하다　　move out 이사를 나가다　　rent 집세, 방세

You Need to Know 2

【1】I wish 가정법

① I wish 가정법 과거
현재의 실현 가능성 없는 소망을 나타낼 때 사용하고 '~라면 좋을텐데'로 해석합니다.

I wish + 주어 + would(could) + 동사원형
I wish + 주어 + 과거동사(be동사일 때는 were)

- I wish somebody would help me. 누군가 날 도와줬음 좋겠는데.
- I wish you were here with me. 네가 여기 나랑 있음 좋을텐데.

② I wish 가정법 과거 완료
과거에 이루어지지 않은 소망과 후회를 나타낼 때 사용하고 '~였다면 좋았을텐데'로 해석합니다.

I wish + 주어 + had p.p.

- I wish the professor had given me the chance. 교수님이 기회를 주셨으면 좋았을텐데.
- I wish I had been nice to my friends. 나의 친구들에게 잘했으면 좋았을텐데.

다음을 우리 말과 같은 뜻이 되도록 문장을 완성하세요.

1. 오늘이 일요일이라면 좋을텐데.
   I __________ __________ __________ Saturday today.
2. 내가 직장을 구한다면 좋을텐데.
   I __________ __________ __________ __________ a job.
3. 내가 차가 있다면 좋을텐데.
   I __________ __________ __________a car.
4. 가격이 낮았더라면 좋았었을텐데.
   I __________ the price __________ __________ lower.
5. 그를 도와줬더라면 좋았었을텐데.
   I __________ I __________ __________ him.

【2】 as if 가정법

① as if 가정법 과거
실제와 다른 상황을 나타낼 때 사용하며, 주절의 시제와 같은 시점의 내용을 나타냅니다. '마치 ~인 것처럼'(실제로는 아님)으로 해석합니다.

as if +	주어 + would(could) + 동사원형
	주어 + 과거동사(be동사일 때는 were)

- Dan always nods his head as if he could understand everything.
  Dan은 항상 마치 그가 모든 것을 이해할 수 있다는 듯 고개를 끄덕인다.
- Miranda talks as if she were my mom.
  Miranda는 그녀가 마치 우리 엄마인 것처럼 말한다.

② as if 가정법 과거완료

실제와 다른 상황을 나타낼 때 사용하며, 주절의 시제보다 더 과거 시점의 내용을 나타냅니다. '마치 ~였던 것처럼'(실제로는 아님)으로 해석합니다.

as if + 주어 + had p.p.

- Jim talked as if he had lived in London.
  Jim은 그가 런던에 살았었던 것처럼 얘기한다.
- Joey looked as if she had loved him.
  Joey는 그를 사랑했었던 것처럼 보인다.

다음을 우리 말과 같은 뜻이 되도록 문장을 완성하세요.

1. 나는 마치 꿈을 꾸고 있는 것 같아.
   I feel __________ __________ I __________ dreaming.
2. 그는 자기가 돈이 많은 것처럼 행동한다.
   He acts __________ __________ he __________ a lot of __________
3. 그들은 마치 서로 사랑하는 것처럼 보인다.
   They look __________ __________they __________ each other.
4. 그는 나에게 전화를 했었던 것처럼 얘기한다.
   He talks __________ __________ he __________ __________ me.
5. 그는 자기가 거기에 있었던 것처럼 말한다.
   He talks __________ __________ he __________ __________ there.

What would you do if … ?

아래의 상황이 벌어진다면 어떻게 하겠습니까? 여러분의 답변을 영어로 써 보세요.

1. What would you do if you saw someone picking pockets in the subway station?

____

____

____

____

2. What would you do if you saw your classmate cheating on an exam?

____

____

____

____

3. What would you do if you won a lottery?

____

____

____

____

친구의 대답과 비교해 보세요.

Wish List

아래 질문의 대답을 완성하여 본인의 Wish List를 만들어 보세요.

Wish List

1. What kind of home do you wish you could live in? ____________
2. What languages do you wish you could speak? ____________
3. What kind of car do you wish you could buy? ____________
4. What kind of job do you wish you could have? ____________
5. What celebrity do you wish you could meet? ____________
6. Which city do you wish you could live in? ____________
7. Which country do you wish you could travel? ____________
8. What kind of person do you wish you could be? ____________
9. Which body part do you wish you could get a cosmetic surgery? ____________
10. What do you wish you could do right now? ____________

친구들의 wish list와 본인의 것을 비교해 보고, 묻고 대답해 봅니다.

A : What kind of home do you wish you could live in?
B : I wish I could live in a house near the beach.
A : Why?
B : I think I could enjoy a great view from home every day.

A. 보기의 동사를 이용하여 가정법 과거 문장을 완성하세요.

go	speak	win	live	like	be	have	can	get	know

1. If I __________ the answer, I would tell you.
2. If Barbara wanted to go out, she'd __________
3. If he __________ the money, he would buy a bag for you.
4. What would you do if you __________ a trip to New York?
5. I wouldn't be there if I __________ you.
6. We'd go to the beach more often if we __________ closer.
7. I'm sorry. I'd help you if I __________
8. It's raining. You'd __________ wet if you went out.
9. She wouldn't take it if she __________ it.
10. I could understand him better if he __________ more slowly.

B. What would you do in these situations?

1. If a classmate asked me to borrow my notebook before exam,
____
2. If I hit someone's car at the parking lot when no one was there,
____
3. If I saw a person begging for money,
____

C. 괄호 안의 동사를 이용하여 가정법 과거완료 문장을 완성하세요.

1. If I ____________ the soccer game, I'd ____________ the ticket.(know / buy)
2. If you ____________ me about the problem, I'd ____________ you.(tell / help)
3. If they ____________, they would ____________ the exam.(study / pass)
4. If I ____________ on the stairs, I wouldn't ____________ my leg.(slip / break)
5. Alex wouldn't ____________ the machine if he ____________ the instruction carefully.(fix / read)

D. 알맞은 동사를 넣으세요.

1. The weather is not good. I wish the weather ____________ right now.
2. I didn't go shopping. I wish I ____________ shopping.
3. I don't know how to cook. I wish I ____________ how to cook.
4. I'm not wearing a coat. I wish I ____________ a coat.
5. I'm busy now. I wish I ____________ go out with you.

E. 알맞은 대답을 골라 보세요.

1. A : I wish I had an easier life.

   B : ____________________

   ① I'm sorry to hear that. Cheer up.

   ② I like my job.
2. A : I wish I could leave this town.

   B : ____________________

   ① Why?

   ② I am leavning.

3. A : I wish I could find a better place.

B : ______________________

① Somewhere else.

② This place is very nice, though.

F. 알맞은 동사를 넣어 아래의 대화를 완성하세요.

Ava I got an offer from the company in Los Angeles.

Emily Great! When are you going?

Ava That's the problem.
What ________ you ________ (do) if your boyfriend asked you not to go?

Emily Well, I __________ (try) to convince him.
That's a very good opportunity for you.

Ava I know.

Emily If I __________ (be) you, I ____________________ (talk) to him.

Martin Luther King Jr.(1929~1968)

아래의 사진은 무엇일까요? 바로 1960년대 중반까지만 해도 미국 곳곳에서 볼 수 있었던 표지판입니다. 이것이 무엇을 의미할까요? 미국의 제 16대 대통령 아브라함 링컨(Abraham Lincoln)이 흑인 노예 해방 선언을 선포한 지100년이 지날 때까지도 미국에서는 피부색에 따른 엄연한 인종 차별이 있었습니다. 흑인들은 피부색이 검다는 이유만으로 버스에서 백인들에게 자리를 양보해야만 했고, 식당에서도 흑인 전용 좌석에서 식사를 해야만 했으며, 백인들이 출입하는 호텔이나 영화관 심지어는 학교에도 가지 못했습니다.

1955년 12월, 로자 파크스(Rosa Parks)라는 흑인 여성이 버스에서 백인 승객에게 자리를 양보해 주지 않아 경찰에 체포되면서 분노에 찬 흑인들이 집단 파업과 버스 보이콧운동을 벌이면서 그 운동을 비폭력 평화주의로 이끌어 온 마틴 루터 킹 목사가 세상에 널리 이름을 알리게 됩니다.

Rosa Parks

그 후 킹 목사는 흑인 인권운동에 관심을 가지며 흑인들의 정치적 권리와 법적 권리, 교육, 문화, 복지후생 등의 면을 옹호하기 위해 노력을 하여 1964년 당시 35세의 나이로 노벨 평화상을 수상하게 됩니다. 하지만 안타깝게도 1968년 백인 우월주의자의 총탄에 암살되고 맙니다. 1986년부터 미국에서는 그를 기려 그의 생일(1월 15일)에 가까운 매년 1월 셋째 주 월요일을 마틴 루터 킹의 날로 정하고 연방정부 공휴일로 지정하였습니다. 킹 목사는 현실감 있는 비유와 수사, 뛰어난 언변을 겸비한 훌륭한 연설가이기도 합니다. 킹 목사의 연설문 중에서도 1963년 8월 28일 워싱턴의 링컨 기념관

Rosa Parks가 앉았던 자리에 앉은 Barack Obama 대통령

광장 앞에서 25만 명의 군중 앞에서 연설한 "I Have a Dream"은 미국의 인권운동사는 물론, 미국역사에 길이 남을 명 연설로 꼽히고 있습니다.

아래는 I Have a Dream 연설문 중 일부만을 발췌한 내용입니다.

I say to you today, my friends, that in spite of the difficulties and frustrations of the moment I still have a dream. It is a dream deeply rooted in the American dream. I have a dream that one day this nation will rise up and live out the true meaning of its creed: "We hold these truths to be self-evident; that all men are created equal."

Martin Luther King Jr.(1929~1968)

나의 친구인 여러분들에게 말씀드립니다. 고난과 좌절의 순간에도, 저는 꿈을 가지고 있다고. 이 꿈은 아메리칸 드림에 깊이 뿌리를 내리고 있는 꿈입니다. 저에게는 꿈이 있습니다. 언젠가 이 나라가 모든 인간은 평등하게 태어났다는 것을 자명한 진실로 받아들이고, 그 진정한 의미를 신조로 살아가게 되는 날이 오리라는 꿈입니다.

I have a dream that one day on the red hills of Georgia the sons of former slaves and the sons of former slave owners will be able to sit down together at the table of brotherhood.
언젠가는 조지아의 붉은 언덕 위에 예전에 노예였던 부모의 자식과 그 노예의 주인이었던 부모의 자식들이 형제애의 식탁에 함께 둘러앉는 날이 오리라는 꿈입니다.

I have a dream that one day even the state of Mississippi, a desert state sweltering the heat of injustice and oppression, will be transformed into an oasis of freedom and justice. I have a dream that my four little children will one day live in a nation where they will not be judged by the color of their skin but by the content of their character.
언젠가는 불의와 억압의 열기에 신음하던 저 황폐한 미시시피주가 자유와 평등의 오아시스가 될 것이라는 꿈입니다. 나의 네 자녀들이 피부색이 아니라 인격에 따라 평가받는 그런 나라에 살게 되는 날이 오리라는 꿈입니다.

I have a dream today. I have a dream that one day the state of Alabama, whose governors lips are presently dripping with the words of interposition and nullification, will be

transformed into a situation where little black boys and black girls will be able to join hands with little white boys and white girls and walk together as sisters and brothers.
오늘 저에게는 꿈이 있습니다. 주지사가 늘 연방정부의 조처에 반대할 수 있다느니, 연방법의 실시를 거부한다느니 하는 말만 하는 앨라배마주가 변하여, 흑인 소년 소녀들이 백인 소년 소녀들과 손을 잡고 형제자매처럼 함께 걸어갈 수 있는 상황이 되는 꿈입니다.

I have a dream that oneday every valley shall be exalted, every hill and mountain shall be made low, the rough places will be made plains, and the crooked places will be made straight, and the glory of the Lord shall be revealed, and all flesh shall see it together.
오늘 저에게는 꿈이 있습니다. 어느날 모든 계곡이 높이 솟아오르고, 모든 언덕과 산은 낮아지고, 거친 곳은 평평해지고, 굽은 곳은 곧게 펴지고, 하느님의 영광이 나타나 모든 사람들이 함께 그 광경을 지켜보는 꿈입니다.

This is our hope. This is the faith with which I return to the South. With this faith we will be able to hew out of the mountain of despair a stone of hope. With this faith we will be able to transform the jangling discords of our nation into a beautiful symphony of brotherhood. With this faith we will be able to work together, to pray together, to struggle together, to go to jail together, to stand up for freedom together, knowing that we will be free one day.
이것이 우리의 희망입니다. 이것이 제가 남부로 돌아갈 때 가지고 가는 신념입니다. 이런 신념을 가지고 있으면 우리는 절망의 산을 개척하여 희망의 돌을 찾아낼 수 있을 것입니다. 이런 희망을 가지고 있으면 우리는 이 나라의 이 소란스러운 불협화음을 형제애로 가득 찬 아름다운 음악으로 변화시킬 수 있을 것입니다. 이런 신념이 있으면 우리는 함께 일하고 함께 기도하며 함께 투쟁하고 함께 감옥에 가며, 함께 자유를 위해 싸울 수 있을 것입니다. 우리가 언젠가 자유로워지리라는 것을 알기 때문입니다.

UNIT 12

Have you ever been to San Francisco?

이번 주에 몇 번이나 아래의 일들을 했습니까?

clean the house

do laundry

go to a club

sing songs with friends

take a walk

친구에게 물어 보세요.

【Example】

Q : How many times have you cleaned the house this week?

A : ____

Conversation 1

Track 23 *Have you been here long?*

Jisu　I'm sorry I'm late. Have you been here long?
Marcos　No, only for a few minutes.
Jisu　How have you been, Marcos? You look good.
Marcos　I've been pretty busy but my final is over now.
So I am quite relaxed.
Jisu　Have you decided the movie yet?
Marcos　No, I can't decide.
Jisu　Hmm. Do you like thriller movies?
Marcos　Actually, I don't.
Jisu　Oh, then, what about comedies?
There's a new Woody Allen movie.
I've seen his movies several times and I liked them.
Marcos　Ok. Let's go.

New Vocabulary

final 기말시험　　several(= some, a few)

You Need to Know 1

【1】 현재완료(Present Perfect)

과거의 어떤 상황이나 행동이 현재에도 영향을 미치고 있거나 관련이 있을 때 현재완료 시제를 사용합니다.

현재완료 평서문

I we you they	have('ve) have not (haven't)	played. lived. visited. read. lost. been. flown.
he she it	has('s) has not (hasn't)	

현재완료 의문문

have	I we you they	played? lived? visited? read? lost? been? flown?
has	he she it	

✔ just, since, so far 등과 같은 시간의 부사(구)와 함께 자주 쓰입니다.

【2】 현재완료 vs. 과거시제

현재완료 시제는 과거에 시작해서 현재까지 계속되는 일을 나타내거나 과거에 일어난 일이 현재까지 영향을 계속 미치는 경우에 쓰입니다. 보통 부사 ever, never, already, just, for, since 등과 함께 쓰입니다.

- I've lived in Seoul for the past ten years.
  지난 10년 동안 서울에서 살았어.(현재도 서울에 있음)
- I have been sick since Monday.
  월요일부터 아팠어.(현재도 아픔)

반면 과거시제는 과거의 어느 시점에 일어난 일이나 상태를 나타낼 때만 씁니다. 현재와의 연관성은 없으며 과거 특정 시점만을 나타내는 부사(구), yesterday, last week, ago, at 1 o'clock 등과 함께 쓰입니다.

- I lived in Seoul 2 years ago.
  2년 전에 서울에서 살았어.(현재는 어디 사는지 모름)
- I was sick yesterday.
  어제 아팠어.(현재는 어떠한지 모름)

다음 밑줄 친 부분을 바르게 고치세요.

1. Peter has lost his watch yesterday. ► ____________________
2. Jasmine have studied French for three years. ► ____________________
3. I didn't have played this game before. ► ____________________
4. He has quit his job two months ago. ► ____________________
5. The police has finished the investigation in 2011. ► ____________________

【3】 already vs. yet

already는 주로 긍정문에서 '이미, 벌써'라는 의미를 가지며 의문문에서는 놀라움을 표현할 때 사용합니다.

- I have already watched the movie. 나는 이미 그 영화를 보았다.
- I've already graduated from high school. 나는 이미 고등학교를 졸업했다.
- Have you already finished your project? (놀라며)프로젝트를 벌써 끝냈어?

yet은 주로 부정문에서 '아직 ~ 않은', 의문문에서 '이미, 벌써'라는 의미로 쓰입니다.

- I haven't watched the movie yet. 나는 아직 그 영화를 보지 못했다.
- I haven't graduated from college yet. 나는 아직 대학을 졸업하지 못했다.
- Have you finished your project yet? 프로젝트를 이미 끝냈니?

밑줄 친 부분에 already나 yet을 쓰세요.

1. Have they eaten dinner ____________?
2. Yes, they've ____________ eaten.
3. No, they haven't eaten ____________

Conversation 2

Track 24 *I've already been there.*

Jisu	Steve, have you ever been to San Francisco?
Steve	Yeah, I've already been there.
Jisu	Wow! When?
Steve	I went there with my family for vacation last year.
Jisu	Great! You can tell me where to go and what to do. Have you visited Fisherman's Wharf?
Steve	Sure. You can find the freshest seafood there. And you'll enjoy shopping at the beautiful marketplace. It's worth taking a visit.
Jisu	Is there anything else I can do there?
Steve	I've taken a ferry to Alcatraz. It was once a prison but it's a tourist attraction now. It has a beautiful garden, too.
Jisu	It all sounds interesting!

New Vocabulary

marketplace 시장, 장터
worth ~할 가치가 있는
prison 교도소, 감옥
tourist attraction 관광지

【1】 현재완료의 용법

① 경험 – 과거부터 현재까지의 경험을 나타낼 때는 현재완료를 사용하며 '~한 적이 있다'의 의미를 나타냅니다. 경험을 나타내는 현재완료는 주로 before, ever, never, once 등과 함께 씁니다.

- I have ever watched that painting. 저 그림을 본 적이 있어요.
- I've visited here to download a new program.
  새 프로그램을 다운받기 위해 여기 방문한 적이 있어요.

② 완료 – 과거의 동작이 현재에 막 완료된 것을 나타내는 현재완료의 용법을 완료용법이라고 하며, '벌써/이미/막 ~했다' 또는 '아직 ~하지 않았다'라는 의미입니다.

- The consultant has just finished the analysis. 컨설턴트가 이제 막 분석을 끝냈다.
- I have already bought his birthday present. 그의 생일선물을 이미 샀어.

③ 계속 – 과거의 어느 시점부터 현재까지 어떤 일이 계속되고 있음을 나타낼 때 현재완료의 계속 용법이라고 하며 '지금까지 계속 ~해 왔다'라는 의미입니다. 주로 for, since, how long 등과 함께 쓰입니다.

- They have been friends for three years. 그들은 3년 동안 친구였다.
- How long have you lived here? 여기서 얼마나 오래 사셨어요?

④ 결과 – 과거의 일로 인해 현재에 어떤 결과가 생겼을 때 현재완료의 결과 용법이라고 하며 '~해 버렸다(그래서 지금은 ~하다)'의 의미입니다. 결과를 나타내는 현재완료는 과거시제와 의미는 같지만, 현재의 상태가 어떤지 알 수 있다는 점에서 과거시제와 구분됩니다.

- Carl has lost his watch. Carl이 시계를 잃어버렸다.(그래서 지금 갖고 있지 않다.)
- Jason has gone to Europe. Jason은 유럽으로 떠났다.(그래서 지금 여기 없다.)

다음의 문장을 우리 말로 옮겨 보세요.

1. Have you ever played chess? ______________________
2. He has gone to meet Brian. ______________________
3. The team has never lost a game. ______________________

【2】 for, since, ago

전치사 for와 since는 동사의 현재완료형과 함께 쓰여 어느 정도의 기간을 나타냅니다. For는 기간(a period of time : ~동안))과 since는 시점(the start of the period : ~부터)을 의미합니다.

for		Since	
three days	a week	Monday	January
an hour	a long time	May 5th	12:30

- Carol has been in Switzerland for five years.
  Carol은 스위스에 5년동안 줄곧 있었다.
- Carol has been in Switzerland since she was 10 years old.
  Carol은 스위스에서 10살 때부터 줄곧 살아왔다.

ago는 과거의 사건(상황)을 표현할 때 쓰며, '(얼마의 시간) 전에'라는 의미입니다. For와 달리 ago는 과거시제에만 쓰입니다.

밑줄 친 부분에 already, yet, for 또는 since 중 맞는 단어를 골라 써보세요.

1. They have __________ finished their dinner.
2. Sarah has traveled Hong Kong __________ 6 days.

3. Good to see you! I haven't seen you __________ your last birthday.

4. Dave hasn't cleaned his room __________.

5. I haven't had this much fun __________ I was a kid.

【3】 현재완료 진행(Present Perfect Progressive)

과거부터 지금까지 계속 하고 있는 일을 이야기할 때 지금 또는 요즘도 하고 있다는 것을 강조하는데 현재완료 진행시제를 씁니다.

- I have been waiting here for 20 minutes. 나는 20분째 기다리고 있다.
- Tom has been reading for 2 hours. Tom은 2시간 째 독서 중이다.

✔ 현재 진행형은 지금 하고 있는 일(상황)에 말의 초점이 맞춰져 있는 반면, 현재완료 진행형은 과거부터 지금까지 해왔던 일(상황)에 초점이 맞추어져 있습니다.

- It's raining now. 지금 비 오네.
- It has been raining for a week. 일주일 째 비가 오고 있어.

✔ 진행형으로 쓸 수 없는 동사(see, know, want, have, love 등)는 현재완료 진행형으로도 쓰일 수 없습니다.

Check up

아래의 문장을 읽고, 현재완료 진행형 문장으로 바꾸어 써 보세요.

1. The boys are playing soccer. They are playing for two hours.

   ► ____

2. Mr. Ford is talking on the phone. He's on the phone for more than an hour.

   ► ____

3. Martin is waiting in the dentist's office. He was waiting for the dentist for the last twenty minutes.

   ► ____

Bingo!

아래 보기를 읽고 빙고 차트에 임의로 숫자를 채우세요.

1. play online games	9. win a lottery
2. borrow money from a friend	10. be on a blind date
3. shop online	11. get into a car accident
4. share a room with a brother or a sister	12. travel alone
5. study past midnight	13. cut your own hair
6. meet famous people	14. fall in love with someone
7. lose wallet	15. try Indian food
8. help stranger	16. be on a TV

파트너와 함께 본인의 경험을 얘기하면서 빙고게임을 합니다. 둘 다 경험해 본 것에는 "O"를, 둘 다 경험해 보지 못했던 것에는 "X"를, 둘 중 한 사람만 경험한 것에는 "Y"를 표시합니다.

Shout "Bingo!" if you are the first person to get four "O"s, "X"s or "Y"s in a straight line.

Have you ever … ?

친구들에게 과거의 경험을 물어 보세요.

lose smart phone   try bungee jump   eat chicken's feet   ride a sports car

【Example】

A : Have you ever lost your smart phone?

B : Yes, I have.

A : Really? Where?

B : I left it on the desk at the library. Unfortunately, I couldn't find it.

여러분이 인터뷰한 친구들 중에서 가장 흥미로운 경험을 한 친구의 얘기를 들려 주세요.

Exercises

A. 현재완료 시제를 사용하여 그림을 묘사해 봅니다. 보기를 이용하세요.

1. before | now

It ______________________

2. before | now

I ______________________

3. before | now

The door ______________________

4.

before | now

The baby ______________________

B. 괄호 안의 단어를 이용하여 현재완료 시제를 만들어 보세요.

1. "__________ (you / ever / play) golf?" "Yes, I play golf a lot."
2. "Does John know Sam?" "No, __________ (he / never / meet) him."
3. Jannifer's favorite book is The Picture. __________ (she / read) it many times.
4. __________ (I / see) that woman before, but I can't remember where.
5. Susan is in Seoul. __________ (she / be) there since Monday.

C. 맞는 표현을 고르세요.

1. Julie (lives / has lived) in Korea since 2012.
2. Diana is a good friend of mine. I (know / have known) her very well.
3. Sorry I'm late. How long (are you / have you been) waiting?
4. How long (do you / have you lived) in this house?
5. Steve (is / has been) in Seattle right now.

D. 본인이 얼마나 자주 아래의 일들을 하는지 보기의 표현을 이용해 문장을 만들어 봅니다.

I've ... many times	I've ... three or four times.
I haven't ... lately	I've never ...

ex) go shopping ► I haven't gone shopping lately.

1. see a movie ► __________
2. call mom ► __________
3. cook dinner ► __________
4. practice guitar ► __________
5. go abroad ► __________

E. 밑줄 친 부분에 문맥에 따라 현재완료 또는 과거 동사를 넣으세요.

1. A : Do you know Jacob's sister?
   B : I ___(1)___ (see) her a few times but I ___(2)___ (never / speak) to her. ___(3)___ (you / ever / speak) to her?
   A : Yes, I ___(4)___ (meet) her at a party last week. She's very nice.

2. Kate works in a factory now, but she ___(1)___ (have) a lot of different jobs. Five year ago, she ___(2)___ (be) a waitress in a restaurant. After that, she ___(3)___ (work) on a ranch, but she ___(4)___ (not / enjoy) it very much.

F. 다음의 우리말을 참고하여 영어로 말해 보세요.

1. 여기서 오래 기다렸니? ______________________________
2. (그동안)어떻게 지냈니? ______________________________
3. (그동안)꽤 바빴어. ______________________________
4. (그동안)그의 영화를 몇 편 봤어요. ______________________________
5. 미국에 가본 적 있니? ______________________________
6. 작년에 가족들이랑 갔었어. ______________________________
7. 어디 가야 할지 말해줄래? ______________________________
8. 뭘 할지 말해줄래? ______________________________
9. 거기서 가장 신선한 해산물을 찾을 수 있어요. ______________________________
10. 한 번 가 볼만한 곳이에요. ______________________________

미국 학생들이 많이 사용하는 구어체 표현

아래의 영어 표현들은 친구들과 얘기할 때는 자연스럽지만, 다른 상황에서는 주의를 필요로 합니다. 미국의 학생들이 친구들과 편안하게 이야기할 때 많이 쓰는 표현들을 정리해 보았습니다.

1. 당근이지. You bet. / Absolutely.
2. 너나 잘 해. None of your business.
3. 뒷북치지 마. Thanks for the history lesson.
4. 어제 필름이 끊겼어. I got blacked out yesterday.
5. 그 사람 그거 참 잘~ 됐다(그게 당연하다). 쌤통이다. He deserves it.
6. 그래, 네 팔뚝 굵다! Okay, You are the boss!

7. 끝까지 가보자! Let's go all the way!
8. 네가 나한테 어떻게 그럴 수 있니? How could you do that to me?
9. 거기 물 좋다. That place rocks! That place kicks!
10. (문제의 답 등이)너무 쉽네. / 얘개 그게 다야? That's it? / Is that all?
11. 너도 내 입장이 되어봐. Put yourself in my shoes.
12. 야, 친구 좋다는 게 뭐야? Come on, what are friends for?
13 미안해 할 것까지는 없어. There's nothing to be sorry about.
14. 이보다 더 좋을 순 없다 It couldn't be better than this!
15. 섭섭(실망)하지 않게 해 드리겠습니다! You won't be disappointed!
16. 나를 만만하게 보지 마. Don't you think I am that easy.(you에 강세)
17. 네가 하는 일이 다 그렇지 뭐. That's what you always do.
18. 분위기 파악 좀 해라, 인간아. Consider your surroundings, you fool.
19. 두고 보자. Just wait! I'll get (또는 pay) you back.
20. 이번 한 번만 봐준다. I'm gonna let it slide only this time.
21. 너무 많은걸 알려고 하면 다쳐. You'll get hurt if you try to know too much.
22. 제발 잘난 척 좀 그만해. Stop acting like you're all that.
23. 장난이 좀 심하군. The joke is too harsh.
24. 말장난 그만 합시다. Let's stop playing word games
25. 내가 만만하게 보여? Do I look like I am easy?
26. 몸이 찌뿌둥하다. I feel heavy
27. 오해하지 마세요. Don't get me wrong.
28. 니 맘대로 하세요. Suit yourself.
29. 아직 옛날실력 안 죽었어. I've still got it.(it은 옛날 실력을 의미)
30. 넌 이제 죽었어! You are dead meat!
31. 너 들으라고 한 소리 아냐. Don't take it personally.
32. 알랑거리지 마. Don't try to butter me up.
33. 배째! Sue me!
34. 그게 어딘데? That's better than nothing?
35. 머리 뚜껑이 열렸다. My head is about to open.
36. 그녀는 이중성격을 가졌어. She has a multi-personality(또는 split personality)
37. (나에게)너무 심한 것 아니예요? Don't you think you are too harsh?
38. 저 사람은 인간이 왜 저래? What's wrong with him?
39. 걔 원래 그런 애야. He's usually like that.

40. 너 삐졌니? Are you mad at me? Are you pissed off?
41. 이 싸가지 없는 녀석아. You have no respect.
42. 그는 밥만 축낸다. You are not worth feeding.
43. 그는 성격이 털털하고 시원시원하다. He has an easy-going and cool attitude.
44. 저애는 내가 찍었어. That boy is mine. He is on my list.
45. 그는 뒤로 호박씨 깐다. He does something in people's back
46. 너무 오버하지 마. Don't go too far.
47. 그냥 그렇다고 해, 뭘 자꾸 따져? Just say it, don't argue
48. 넌 왜 맨날 그 모양이니? Why are you always like that?
49. 뭐 이런 사람이 다 있어~! What kind of person is this!
50. 너 미쳤니? / 너 제 정신이야? Are you crazy or something?
51. 어휴~ 난 이제 죽었다. Man. I'm dead now.
52. 그 여자는 너무 코가 높아 (콧대가 세다 / 도도하다). She's too snobby.
53. 내 일은 내가 알아서 다 할 거야. I'll take care of my business.
54. 뭐 찔리는 거라도 있는 거야? Are you hiding something?
55. 너 시치미 떼지 마. Don't you try to lie. (you에 강세)
56. 좋은 사람 있으면 소개시켜 줘. Hook me up if there's a good person.
57. 누가 네 성격을 받아주겠니. Who would put up with your attitude?
58. 결코 고의가 아니었다. I didn't mean to do that. / It's not what I mean.
59. 넌 배신자다. You are a traitor!
60. 다 티 난다. Everything shows./ It's too obvious. / You can't hide it.

현재	과거	과거분사	현재	과거	과거분사
am, are, is	was, were	been	lose	lost	lost
become	became	become	make	made	made
begin	begen	begun	mean	meant	meant
bring	brought	brought	pay	paid	paid
build	built	built	put	put	put
buy	bought	bought	read	read	read
choose	chose	chosen	ride	rode	ridden
cost	cost	cost	run	ran	run
do	did	done	say	said	said
draw	drew	drawn	see	saw	seen
drink	drank	drunk	sell	sold	sold
drive	drove	driven	send	sent	sent
eat	ate	eaten	show	showed	shown
fall	fell	fallen	sing	sang	sung
feel	felt	felt	sit	sat	sat
fly	flew	flown	sleep	slept	slept
find	found	found	speak	spoke	spoken
forget	forgot	forgot	stand	stood	stood
get	got	got, gotten	swim	swam	swum
go	went	gone	take	took	taken
grow	grew	grown	teach	taught	taught
give	gave	given	tell	told	told
have, has	had	had	think	thought	thought
hear	heard	heard	throw	threw	thrown
hide	hid	hidden	understand	understood	understood
hold	held	held	wear	wore	worn
hurt	hurt	hurt	win	won	won
keep	kept	kept	write	wrote	written
know	knew	known			
leave	left	left			
let	let	let			
light	lit	lit			

REFERENCES

안소영, 능률영어교육연구소, 『문제로 마스터하는 중학 영문법』, 능률교육(2011).

유현정, Davis J, 『New English 900 기초 영문법』, YBM(2013).

윤석철, 『Ok Grammar』, 넥서스 에듀(2008).

파고다 언어교육연구소, 『Talk Talk』, 위트앤위즈덤(2008).

Azar B. 2006. Understandning and Using English Grammar. New York. Pearson Longman.

MacKay S., Sherman K., Forstrom J., Pitt M., Velasco S. 2008. Excellent English. New York. McGraw Hill.

Murphy R., Smalzer W. 2002. Basic Grammar in Use. New York. Cambridge.

Richards J, Hull J., Proctor S. 2008. Interchange 3rd Ed. New York. Cambridge.

【사진출처】

Photos.com

tx.english-ch.com

nycgo.com